Jeanine
Johnson

Tara's Angels

Tara's Angels

One Family's
Extraordinary Journey of
Courage and Healing

Kirk Moore

H J KRAMER
TIBURON, CALIFORNIA

H J Kramer Inc
P.O. Box 1082
Tiburon, CA 94920

Editor: Nancy Grimley Carleton
Editorial Assistant: Claudette Charbonneau
Cover Design: Jim Marin/Marin Graphic Services
Composition: Classic Typography
Book Production: Schuettge & Carleton
Manufactured in the United States of America.
10 9 8 7 6 5 4 3 2 1

Library of Congress Cataloging-in-Publication Data
Moore, Kirk, 1952–
    Tara's angels : one family's extraordinary journey of courage and
healing / by Kirk Moore.
        p. cm.
    Includes bibliographical references.
    ISBN 0–915811–67–7
    1. Angels. 2. Moore, Tara Lauren, 1977–1992. 3. Moore, Kirk,
1952–   . 4. Spiritual healing. 5. Spiritual biography.
I. Title.
BL477.M66   1996
291.2'15—dc20   95–46941
                                                              CIP

To my wife and soul mate, Sandy,
and my beloved daughter, Deanna.

Contents

Foreword

In the autumn of 1992, I was leading a workshop on angels in Los Angeles. Two of the participants immediately caught my eye as they entered the room. I noticed their angel T-shirts, which at the time were rare to see, but mostly I noticed the extraordinary light they were radiating. I was also struck by the fact that one of them was so young, but so wise looking, spiritually confident, and beautiful for her age.

After the workshop, they came over to me and handed me a copy of *Messengers of Light,* the first book I'd written. This particular copy had developed a personality all its own. Some of the pages were curled in from use. It had the flexibility of a well-read book. They asked me to sign the book to Tara, the young girl's older sister, who had recently been killed in a car accident. Then the lovely woman who had escorted the young girl began to tell me a story I will never forget. That story is in this book, so I need not tell you it now. It is a story you will not forget. In fact, it will become a part of you in a very healing way.

I was amazed by what I had heard. I cannot imagine how I must have seemed to the two of them, but they both had such a wonderful strength and love about them that I felt they would understand and accept me no matter what. I remember being beyond tears, but my heart was flooded with a mixture of emotions that I knew would emerge later. Somehow I signed the book to Tara, and they left. I was speechless (which is rare), and luckily my friend Shannon had been standing nearby listening and knew that something very profound had taken place, so I had a witness to help me process the information.

About a week after the workshop, I tried to find a way to reach them. I got out the list of participants, but I couldn't figure out who they were from the list. I tried a few other avenues but had no luck in tracking them down. I wanted to keep in touch and know more about how the angels would help them and if I could be of help in any way. I finally gave up, thinking to myself that in time maybe the angels would help us cross paths again.

Tara and her family were often in my prayers. One day in early 1994, I was sitting with my computer trying to get the inspiration to write one more meditation for a book I was currently behind in writing. I began to think strongly about Tara. I wondered about who she is now and thought about her short time here on the planet. I cried a little, and then the image of a most beautiful comet flashed through my mind. I thought about how comets come through the sky, only giving us enough time to feel awe at their beauty and then mysteriously leaving us with memories and the sense that we've been touched in a profound way. So I wrote a meditation on comets and dedicated it to Tara. Then I prayed that she would go on sharing her brilliant light, and I asked the angels to just let me know how her family was doing.

Well, the next day I received a phone message from an excited friend, who told me about a special angel store she had come across. She told me that the store was named after a girl who had died, and that my book had been very important to this girl, and that the name of the girl was Tara. I knew right away exactly whom she was talking about, and I thanked God and the angels for answering my prayer.

Soon after this, Rex Hauck called me to discuss the TV project he was doing on angels. I adamantly told him I thought he should call the people who had opened a store called Tara's Angels. Again, you will read about this in this book, so I need not tell you more now.

I feel very honored to be writing this foreword. I knew that reading this book would not be easy for me, and I imagined I would choose a time to read it when I was feeling strong and centered. Funny, but the book chose the time for me to read it, and I wasn't feeling strong and centered. Instead, I was in one of my "sad for the soul of the world" moods. I don't even remember why I picked the manuscript up in this mood, but as soon as I did, I couldn't put it down.

There is one cure for the ills of the world, and that is love. Love isn't always easy, and we often wonder why we volunteer to venture deeply into love when it has the potential to cause pain. Love is why we exist, and this book will remind you of that because it is written from the heart of someone who chose to do one of the most courageous things a human can do: stay awake and conscious of his pain, then tell his story, creating something beautiful and healing from his experience. Kirk Moore has set forth a new possibility of God's love, something we are all here to do in our own special way. It is not an easy task. By sharing his story so beautifully and truthfully, Kirk has sent forth a pattern of healing that people can follow and then branch off in their own new healing pattern.

Kirk, Sandy, Deanna, and Tara Moore confirm everything I have ever written about angels and the spiritual path of humans. I thank Kirk for sharing his way of being, because he is an inspiration, a breath from God. People are currently seeking information about what happens to us when we die and when our loved ones die.

We want to know about the spiritual help available to us in the form of angels. And we are curious about how families can survive and thrive in the midst of all the craziness experienced right now on the planet.

Answers are wonderful and beautiful, but I think questions are even better. Questions propel us. We need them to keep us alive and inspired. The answers to these questions then lead us to expand our knowing and find new questions. Answers are examples of God's possibilities, and when we go beyond our answers, we will find our own truths. This book touches on universal questions and generously gives us possibilities. It reassures us that death is not a punishment and life is not a prison term. We are here to help the angels keep love alive. We are here to evolve into a glorious possibility of God. We have free will, which means choice. This book is one of the best examples of how one life can help transform and heal others when we choose to do God's will. Thank you, Kirk. Thank you, Sandy. Thank you, Deanna. And thank you, Tara.

—Terry Lynn Taylor
Author of *Messengers of Light*

Preface

We are all here on Earth for a purpose. No matter how large or how small, we each have a reason for being here. It is through our greatest tragedies that we have the opportunity to make our most significant growth. If we can look at each experience in life as a lesson and learn from it, we can continue to evolve into the perfect spirit that God has created. Life is a very precious gift that is passed on to us for only a moment in time. Love it, cherish it, and don't ever take it for granted, for it can be taken away as quickly as it was created. Change the things that you cannot accept, and accept the things that you cannot change. For as life unfolds, the journey of one's soul begins and living becomes a series of miracles.

—Kirk Moore
Winter 1996

Acknowledgments

There is one person I wish to acknowledge in particular for the ideas and beliefs that I have come to know and live—the Reverend Dr. Jackie Harrold. Her understanding of the universe and her ability to impart this knowledge and wisdom to others has enabled me to understand my journey. She has demonstrated that life is an exciting adventure, and she has added clarity and understanding to that journey. She knows how life works. She won't move mountains or find rainbows for you, but she will give you the tools and the means to do this for yourself, which makes the process all the more valuable. Dr. Jackie has loved and supported the four of us and now the three of us in this adventure called life, and she has become an integral part of our family. She is a gift from God.

This book is dedicated to the two most important and loving people in my life. I praise and commend my wife Sandy, who is my soul mate and has loved me and supported me in my journey—our journey—through life. She has demonstrated the strength a soul must have to endure the challenges of the human experience. Her greatest attribute is her devotion to helping others in achieving their highest potential with love and acceptance. Sandy looks for the good in everyone. Her choice to spend this lifetime with me and experience these events is truly courageous.

This book is also dedicated to my exceptional daughter, Deanna—a miracle on earth. Deanna has so much wisdom and love; she creates joy in my life the way nothing else can. She is a very special soul with a very special mission of her own, and she will make a big difference to our planet. She, too, has chosen to overcome the greatest hardship anyone should have to endure. Her path in life will only make her stronger and encourage others to attain their dreams. She has been an inspiration to me. I love her with all my heart.

The three of us are now joined at the hip. Through our experience, we have melded together as one and have come to learn that we are each a part of the whole.

I feel we can all learn something from other people's experience. I thank God and the universe for allowing me to be a vehicle for getting a message out to as many people as possible.

1

The Beginning
of the Divine Plan

Place yourself in the arms of God
and the angels.
They will support you
and guide you in the lessons you need to learn
along your journey in life.

Somehow I always knew that life was like a jigsaw puzzle and that my quest was to see how all the pieces were connected. I believe that God has a greater plan for each of us, and our inner wisdom can interlock all the pieces.

During the summer of 1961, something occurred that would change my perception of my purpose here on Earth. From somewhere above, I was observing a dramatic scene unfold in a parklike backyard surrounded by huge pepper trees. A woman in a pink dress was struggling to answer a police officer's questions. Her voice was quivering, and she was trying to respond through the tears streaming down her face. An ambulance entered the driveway, and I saw a nine-year-old boy lying on the ground, motionless, unconscious, and covered with blood. The detail with which I saw this scene was incredible— right down to the tiny gray stripes on the woman's pink dress. The ambulance sped away with the boy and his mother by his side.

This scene would remain in my mind throughout my life. The woman was my mother, and I was the nine-year-old boy lying on the ground. The interesting part was having viewed the scene from twenty or thirty feet above the ground.

I was finally revived at the hospital with no recollection of what had occurred between the time the ambulance sped away and the time I woke up. I found out that I had suffered a concussion and had received twenty-two stitches in my back—all from a thirty-foot fall from a tree. I was released from the hospital about a week later and spent the rest of the summer recovering. Somehow, my brush with death had created a new dimension in my life. At nine years old, I had a strong inner knowing that my life had been altered forever. I now knew that I had a purpose and a mission. Oddly enough, I never questioned this awareness at such a young age; I just accepted it.

During the next thirteen years, various thoughts and desires would enter my mind that held a certain importance, almost as if I were being given a glimpse of events to come. I remember thinking on many occasions that I wanted to marry someday and have children. In retrospect, it seems odd that at nine, ten, and eleven years old I would be thinking of the importance of marriage as a central purpose in my life, but once again, this would become clearer later. However, a sense of certainty about my future was always with me.

My parents divorced when I was fifteen due to my father's severe battle with alcoholism. My two older brothers had already left home, and one day my father left, too. That was the last I saw of him until I was eighteen. It wasn't until about fifteen years later that I was able to forgive him for deserting my mother and me. My father and I never established a close bond of any kind, but we did speak to each other a couple of times each year. My mother, on the other hand, always furnished me with the love and support that I needed so much during my adolescent years.

Since I was four years old, music has always played a major role in my life. I received a piano for my fourth birthday and never stopped playing from that day forward. My mother was very supportive of my passion for music, and no matter what our financial situation was, she made sure that I was able to maintain my music lessons and studies. She recognized the importance that music played in my life.

Throughout my teenage years, I could sense the deep pain my mother was harboring inside. However, she had a way of masking her pain from others. She was a strong woman and encouraged me to do whatever made me happiest. She often told me, "You can do anything you want to do if you just put your mind to it." The strength and conviction of her words would ring throughout my life and bring me closer to my own power. I thank God for my mother's courage and dedication to life.

I went through my teenage years and into my early twenties with a perpetual sense of being different from my peers, but I tried hard to fit in. I always felt alone, although I was very social, and I had learned to be self-sufficient and very independent. It was very important to me after I graduated from high school to move out on my own and support myself while attending college. I felt I had something to prove, although I didn't know what. I developed a love for acting and performing while maintaining a reclusive side when I wasn't acting. I wanted to love and be loved in my relationships, but I could never grasp the deep, sincere feeling of closeness I longed for. I was looking for the "right" someone to be with—someone who was a friend, someone who was supportive and unconditionally loving, someone whom I could love naturally and be myself with.

In 1973, at age twenty-one, I met Sandy while I was playing with my band in a local nightclub. Sandy had entered the teaching profession after graduating from U.S.C. She appeared to have been drawn into teaching through natural instinct. With no encouragement from anyone outside, she followed her heart and embarked on her career. Her tendency to nurture everyone and everything was probably her strongest characteristic. As a teacher, Sandy's goal was to build her students' self-esteem and make learning enjoyable. Every student she taught had a positive experience from being in her class. Teaching was not just a job for Sandy, but her purpose in life. I truly believe that she was put on the planet to guide and support others. She had a way of making people feel good about themselves and encouraging them to be the best people they could be. Sandy had practically grown up as an only child. Her only other sibling was eleven years her senior.

Sandy would often come to the club where my band played, along with the mutual friends who had introduced us. We became very good friends and remained that way for quite some time. We would often discuss the relationships we were each involved in and the frustrations that accompanied these relationships. Our friendship was a very deep and understanding one, unlike any other either one of us had experienced. We would look forward to each other's company and eagerly share the ups and downs of our current dating ordeals. We would try to console each other with solutions from the opposite perspective. Because we met when we were each dating others and then became close friends, we had never really considered dating each other.

Our first semi-official date was in September 1974, over a year after we met. We were going to the Los Angeles County Fair with the couple who had introduced us. It was a very hot day, and I was wearing white bell bottom pants and a white shirt since I knew that white helped to reflect the heat and could potentially keep me cooler than wearing darker colors. The four of us took a break from the exhibits to have lunch, and I ordered two cheese enchiladas. No sooner was I served than I picked up the plate, lost my balance, and spilled the enchiladas, covered with red sauce, all over my white clothing. This made a lasting impression on Sandy, who couldn't understand why anyone would wear all white to a county fair in the first place! After everyone tried to help me rid my clothes of this mess, we all had a good laugh and enjoyed the rest of the day. Sandy didn't seem embarrassed to be seen with me looking ridiculous; we just made light of the situation and continued our conversation. But, even though we had had a good time, I knew that Sandy was currently seeing someone else.

Then one evening shortly after our day together, I began to realize what was going on in my heart and my mind. My band was performing in a somewhat upscale lounge, and in walked Sandy with her current boyfriend. They sat at a table fairly close to the stage. Ironically, the next song we were performing was "I Honestly Love You." I was completely unaware of my attentiveness to Sandy while I was playing this love song. After the song was completed, Sandy's boyfriend asked her if she was aware of how I had looked into her eyes and how she had returned the gaze. He continued to observe, in a casual manner, that there was something going on between the two of us. When Sandy shared this conversation with me later, I was not yet aware of anything such as this going on—at least not consciously.

Sandy's boyfriend's comments that evening caused me to ponder my true intentions and feelings. Maybe there was a deeper connection that went beyond friendship between me and Sandy that neither of us had acknowledged. We didn't discuss the evening any further after that, but my heart could not deny the fact that I was deeply in love with Sandy. We were both still dating others, but I know how I felt. I was afraid to express my true feelings to Sandy. The love I felt for her was like no other passion I had ever experienced. I guess I was afraid of her reaction and the possible rejection that I would experience if I were to tell her that I had fallen in love with her. I had placed Sandy on a pedestal, and I didn't entertain the thought that she might possibly have the same feelings for me.

Over the next few months, I battled with the idea of expressing my feelings to Sandy verbally. Meanwhile, our relationship remained as it had been—a very deep and trusting friendship. One evening she offered to make me one of my favorite dinners, shish-kebab. The evening started out with a few glasses of wine, then dinner, accompanied by more wine, and then a couple of glasses of wine after dinner. I was the one drinking all the wine. Having consumed so much alcohol, I lost all inhibitions about what I was to blurt out. "Sandy, I have to tell you something." I stopped at that. Sandy said, "Go ahead, what is it?" With one deep breath I said, "I...I love you!" There was a piercing silence as I closed my eyes and waited for something, anything, to happen. Sandy's response was, "I think you're just confused right now." This was not the response I had hoped for, so I repeated myself. "No, I really love you! I know how I feel." Sandy casually changed the subject, and I felt like a total fool, making the rest of the evening somewhat uncomfortable. I moved to the sofa and realized that I was dozing off due to the amount of wine I had drunk. I must have been making quite an impression!

Sandy and I did not speak of the events of that evening until something occurred in November 1974. Sandy decided that she wanted to move to an apartment on the beach, where perhaps she could meet a "nice young man" and eventually get married. I, of course, offered to help her move. The apartment was tiny but right on the beach next to the pier in Redondo Beach. We finished the move late in the evening, and I could no longer bear the silence I had been maintaining. After everything was in its place, I grabbed Sandy and looked her in the eyes and said, "I love you! Either I move in here with you, or we get married; which will it be?" Sandy didn't quite know what to say except, "Well, I don't know. I'll have to think about this." But Sandy could no longer deny her feelings. The next day she accepted my somewhat demanding marriage proposal.

We later discovered that our paths had been crossing for some eighteen years prior to our engagement. In 1957 there was a children's television show filmed in Hollywood, California. The premise was that two children who were having a birthday could each invite ten of their friends to appear on *Chucko the Birthday Clown* for games and a party. Sandy and I were both on that show as guests of the two birthday children. Our paths had also crossed in 1963, when we had both spent the summer with our families at Bass Lake in California. I grew up in Torrance, California, and Sandy grew up in Brentwood, California. In 1966, her family moved to Torrance, and we both attended South High School. Although we never met in high school, she enrolled in a speech class right next door to the drama class that I had enrolled in. I'm sure we passed each other daily while going to and from class. I later found out that my older brother knew Sandy through his best friend. For some reason, our close encounters were not to be consummated for several years, but it was evident that we were destined to be part of each other's lives.

After about a year and a half of adjusting to married life, Sandy and I decided we were ready to have children. Having a family was something that was extremely important to both of us. Within just three short months of making this decision, Sandy was with child. Sandy continued teaching up to two weeks prior to giving birth, while I struggled with my unfulfilling job and continued teaching piano. With each month that passed, I became more excited at the opportunity of being a father. The miraculous thought of Sandy and me creating a new being and bringing it into this world was all consuming.

We attended natural childbirth classes because I planned to be present at the birth of our first child. Sandy and I could hardly wait for the special day when she would go into labor and we could put all that we had learned into practice. Unfortunately, Sandy developed a complication with the pregnancy just a week prior to her due date that required the doctor to reconsider a natural delivery. He said that Sandy would have to deliver the baby via a cesarean section. This was the safest way to proceed for both her and the baby. We were both extremely disappointed by this news. I remember we sat on the floor together crying because this was not what we had intended and I would not be able to be present at the birth. We knew this was what was best for both Sandy and the baby, so we proceeded to adjust to the change in plans.

The surgery was scheduled, and I waited and paced as all expectant fathers do. I was more concerned with Sandy's well-being than anything else. It felt like days went by as I waited for the doctor to appear. Finally, the doctor came out and told me that Sandy was doing fine and that I had a new baby daughter. I said, "Are you sure it's a girl?" Not that I was at all disappointed, but for some reason Sandy and I had thought we were having a boy. I was relieved and excited all at the same time, and very proud. Here it was, June 7, 1977, and our first child, Tara Lauren Moore, was born into our lives. She was an absolutely beautiful soul, a gift from God, a blessing in our existence. Sandy and I had chosen the name Tara because of its meaning in *Gone With the Wind*.

Sandy developed a sudden infection that forced her to remain in the hospital for a week. The most difficult part was that she was not allowed to see Tara. The doctors were concerned because the infection was highly contagious. Sandy had given birth to Tara, but she had not even seen or touched her new baby since the birth. I was visiting them both as much as possible, assuring Sandy that Tara was doing just fine. Tara was placed in an incubator for observation during the first few days.

After Sandy had been in the hospital about three days, I was visiting her when she awoke from a nap. I had just seen Tara, and I had shared how beautiful Tara was and how proud we should be for producing such a gorgeous child. Sandy was thrilled to hear this, but she wanted to see her newborn so badly. She suddenly became concerned that something awful had happened to Tara and that I, along with the hospital staff, was trying to protect her. I assured Sandy that Tara was fine and that the doctors were doing what was best for Tara's health. Sandy would not listen. Her mind was conjuring up needless fears. She demanded to see Tara. Her voice was becoming more hysterical sounding as panic set in. She started raising her voice, saying that something had happened to her baby, and she pleaded for some response immediately. "I need to see Tara! I want to see my baby! Something has happened to her. Please let me see her now!" Sandy was insistent.

I was finally able to calm Sandy and convince her that Tara was doing fine and that there was nothing to worry about. Still, it was a very difficult situation for Sandy not to be able to see her new daughter.

After five long days, Sandy and Tara were released from the hospital, and Sandy could finally see and hold Tara for the first time. The joy that emanated from Sandy's face brought tears streaming down my face. The three of us headed for home, and as I ushered Sandy and Tara through the door of our home, I had a record playing. It was "Tara's Theme" from *Gone With the Wind*. The love that radiated among the three of us was incredible. I could finally experience firsthand the love a parent has for a child and the unconditional love of a child toward her parents. The new awareness and experience would be with my soul forever.

Life moves like the ebb and flow of the tide. Along with this gift of new life, an unfortunate tragedy struck our lives at the same time. My mother, who had been diagnosed with cancer nine months prior to Tara's birth, was blessed with seeing her first grandchild. Somehow, through her powerful will, my mother was able to live to witness this miracle. She passed away one month after Tara's birth, which left me in shock. I was only twenty-five, and I had thought that my mother was immortal and would overcome this disease. I felt confused, lonely, and angry, and I regretted that I never got to tell her how much I loved her and that I was unable to say good-bye. Feeling such joy at Tara's birth and sorrow at my mother's death truly presented a dichotomy. I questioned God about life and death; I thanked God, on the one hand, for the joy of a new life, but I also asked why a life was taken from me at such an important time. All of these experiences would eventually make sense, but at the time they just seemed like hurdles. However, the sense of purpose was still in the forefront of my mind, inspiring me to reach the pivotal point in my life where all questions would be answered.

My mother had left my two brothers and me with a small insurance policy and a legacy of how to live a positive life. With the six thousand dollars I received, Sandy and I decided that my mother would have wanted us to try to purchase a home for the three of us. This wasn't much money, even in 1977, but we did find a house just around the corner from where I was born in 1952. We moved into the house in September and began painting and wallpapering to make this a warm and welcome home. It was a very small house, consisting of only two small bedrooms and one bath, but it was perfect for our needs. We felt very comfortable in our new home and with our new family, although I continued missing my mother very much and was brokenhearted that she was not able to enjoy her first grandchild.

About three months later, I had an experience that I kept inside me for some time, not even sharing it with Sandy. I had been feeling no closure or completion with my mother since her death. I felt angry that she had been taken from me so early in my life and in her life; she was only fifty-two when she died. She had always wanted grandchildren, and especially a granddaughter, since her three children were boys. I was saddened by the fact that she would not get to see her granddaughter grow up and that my children would be cheated out of the wonderful experience of knowing my mother.

Then one night I had a dream, actually a vision. There

is a real difference between the two, and perhaps only if you have experienced a vision can you differentiate the two. While sleeping (being in an unconscious state of mind), my soul or spirit left my body and floated high in the sky and through the heavens above, connected to my body only by a thin silver cord. I was not aware of what this cord was, as I had never done any research in this area of metaphysics. Then my mother met me on the other side and shared with me how happy she was and told me there was nothing to fear. She looked healthy and extremely content. I told her how much I loved and appreciated her. She said that there was nothing but love in her existence now and that she would always be with me. I had felt that my mother had left this Earth early because of her unhappiness and suffering; she had never really gotten over my father leaving. She was a very strong and independent woman but kept many of her feelings and anger locked up inside, which I feel resulted in her developing cancer. Just before I drifted back into my body, my mother said good-bye and told me how proud she was of me.

When I awoke the next morning, I felt as though I had been healed. My sorrow was gone, and feelings of joy and hope were saturating my entire body. Everything that occurred that night was so vivid in my mind. I kept trying to tell myself that maybe it was all a dream. But the feelings were too real, and I felt completely renewed. There was no doubt in my mind about what had happened. I wanted to share my experience with Sandy, but I was not yet comfortable being open about this extraordinary journey. Sandy noticed a change in me afterward, but she did not know what to attribute it to. About five or six months later, while I was traveling to San Diego, I finally decided to share my experience with Sandy. She believed me and marveled at what had taken place and the way it had changed me. I now know that the angels supporting me on my journey and spiritual path were responsible for this divine intervention. I was ready for this experience, and I needed it to move forward. The feeling of that experience will always remain with me.

2

A Vision of Destiny

We are each God's unique gift to the world,
and we are here on purpose,
to share and express our talents.

As Tara began to grow, we sensed her uniqueness. She was always very busy, and her feet were never planted very firmly on the ground. She appeared to be wise beyond her years. She seemed to appreciate every person she met, and she possessed a gift of joy.

Tara's first year of life was a great learning experience for Sandy and me. Tara did not like to sleep as much as most babies. I got the impression that she was afraid she was going to miss out on something. She wanted to be awake with us and to spend time just experiencing life at this fragile age. Whether we knew it or not, she was teaching us about love and joy on a new level just by being in our lives. We took Tara everywhere because she was so social. She always enjoyed laughing. She loved people and was very aware of what was going on around her. We always said that Tara was an adult in an infant's body.

It didn't take long for us to realize that this was just the beginning of our family. Sandy and I knew we wanted more children, as many as we could afford, but with my meager salary and her teacher's salary, it was difficult. God does work in mysterious ways and seems to make the decisions that we can't seem to make. In June 1979, we discovered that Sandy was pregnant. I was surprised but overjoyed at the thought of having a second child. God does know what is best for each of us and always has a good sense of timing.

Sandy, again, taught school all through her pregnancy. We were prepared for another cesarean section because the doctors did not recommend a natural birth for a woman who had had a C-section previously. However, this time I was allowed to be in the room with Sandy during the procedure.

Just a month prior to the birth, my grandmother on my mother's side passed away. She had lived with my mom and dad and brothers and me for several years. I tried once again to understand the correlation between life and death. I think my grandmother, too, died of a broken heart over losing her daughter (my mother) just two and a half years before. Somehow it seemed I was being presented with a lesson about overcoming loss and dealing with grief. Unfortunately, these experiences were causing me to build walls and lose trust. I suppose that this was my mechanism for dealing with the hurt and the pain. I attempted to focus my attention on the more positive experience that lay ahead of me—the birth of my second child.

On February 6, 1980, Tara's sister, Deanna Ashley Moore, was born—another gift from heaven. This time I was there to witness it. Deanna was very different from Tara in that she had her feet much more firmly planted on the ground. God has a way of giving each individual his or her own unique gifts. We were blessed with two such unique beings. As different as Tara and Deanna were, they soon became the best of friends. I remember very vividly bringing Deanna home from the hospital. She had a look of wonderment on her face much the way a koala does. Sandy's mother, Helen, was there, helping Sandy recuperate after her second C-section. Helen suggested that Tara sit on the sofa and hold her new baby sister, and I took a photograph of Tara, Deanna, and

Helen. I snapped the picture, and Helen reached over to retrieve Deanna from Tara's arms. Before Helen could grab onto Deanna, Tara abruptly bit Helen's toe. It was nothing severe, just a gentle, little action that Sandy and I took as a small indication of jealousy over the new family addition. We tried to hold back the laughter as we scolded Tara for biting Helen's toe. But as I thought more about this episode, I began to realize that, perhaps, Tara was being protective of Deanna and did not want her taken away. For this was to be Tara's pattern over the next several years as she and Deanna grew together and watched over each other. There was pure admiration between the two of them—not that they didn't have their differences, but they respected and appreciated each other to the fullest. Sandy and I now felt we had the perfect family. We were all so close, and our life centered around one another. We had difficult times as many people do, but I always held on to the thought that no matter what happened, I had my family and nothing could ever take that away.

As Tara and Deanna grew through their toddler years, their bond continued to strengthen. Tara seemed to be the teacher, and Deanna was eager to learn from her.

Tara developed imaginary friends, as many children do, and insisted that they come with us wherever we went. Deanna was always in agreement with Tara, as she looked up to her older sister for guidance and comfort.

As time went by, the four of us were inseparable and shared a bond that only the closest of families can experience. One of Tara's favorite things was to have the four of us hold hands in a circle and, in the fashion of ring-around-the-rosy, chant, "We love each other." This made us all beam from ear to ear as we repeated the words over and over. Tara and Deanna loved to play dress-up and to sing and dance while I took endless videos of them performing.

Over time, we became aware that Tara often had difficulty completing a task. Her mind was such that she could not stay focused on just one thing at a time. She wanted to do everything all at the same time, which is humanly impossible, but she still tried. She laughed and was always looking to have fun. She insisted on being around people, never alone. People's emotions and learning about life seemed to be the most important things to Tara.

Deanna, on the other hand, was always very task oriented and extremely focused on anything she put her mind to. Unlike Tara, she completed everything she started, and with the utmost perfection. Deanna truly took pride in everything she became involved in. Deanna had a natural love and understanding for people and developed a great compassion for the human race, animals, and the environment. I always knew that Deanna had a mission on the planet and that she, too, would have to face challenges in order to accomplish her purpose.

In 1982, Tara started kindergarten. We discovered that Tara had an attention deficit disorder and that she was hyperactive. This explained her constant busyness and her inability to remain focused on a task. A teacher recommended that we control her hyperactivity through the use of medication. Based on a doctor's evaluation, we proceeded to medicate her. Her teacher said she saw a significant improvement in Tara's schoolwork. We hated the thought that Tara was having to rely on this medication, but at that time there seemed to be no other alternative, and most of the results were positive.

Our life seemed to be centered around learning from both Tara and Deanna. Both Sandy and I truly loved and enjoyed every minute we spent with our children. Tara and Deanna were the joy of our life, and the connection the four of us shared had created a deep bond. My focus in life became the four of us. Children are truly a gift from God, and the growth that we can all gain from them is beneficial for our own evolution.

In 1985 a fad erupted that both Tara and Deanna became enthusiastic about: the Cabbage Patch Doll.

Christmas that year was the beginning of what became an overwhelming collection of these dolls. During the next year the two of them would receive over twenty-three dolls as gifts, and they would play with them for hours. Each doll had a name and a birthday. They held tea parties, birthday parties, weddings, and other celebrations. They loved their new friends and would take two or three of them wherever they went.

In other respects, I found it amazing how two children from the same family could have such different interests and personalities. I'm sure it is because we each come into this experience with a unique purpose and mission in life. Tara was always the more serious child and would tend to take control of a situation. Deanna was extremely comical and wanted to make people laugh as much as possible. Deanna was a much easier child, and Tara was more demanding and had certain expectations about things. As different as they were, they complemented each other because of their differences. There was never any competition or jealousy between them. They looked to each other for the strengths that they lacked, and they understood each other's weaknesses while encouraging each other to overcome them. They were special. Our family was special.

Every birthday had a theme and was a big event. There were circus themes, Disney themes, an Olympic theme in 1986, and once a farm theme, featuring an array of animals. Halloween was always fun: When Tara was an angel, Deanna was a devil. When Tara was a princess, Deanna was a pea. When Tara was Alice in Wonderland, Deanna was the White Rabbit. When Tara was Little Bo Peep, Deanna was a sheep. When Tara was a cavewoman, Deanna was a dinosaur. One year Tara was a Cabbage Patch Doll, and Deanna got to be a Cabbage Patch Doll, too. These were the best years of our life.

As Tara grew older, Sandy and I felt that she was destined to do something important in this world. She loved acting and modeling and was evolving into a beautiful young girl. She was not an easy child by any means. She was headstrong and powerful and had a mind of her own. She was extremely busy and continued to have difficulty remaining focused on one task at a time due to her hyperactivity and attention deficit disorder. In an attempt to wean her off medication, we tried changing her diet to eliminate sugar and unnatural substances. We also tried playing soothing music at night before she went to bed. Our attempts were futile.

During this time of searching, we received an invitation to a social function featuring Karen, a woman who worked with people to assist them in healing. Karen was also a metaphysician and a psychic healer. Sandy and I had never seen a psychic or someone who works with energy, and we thought it would be interesting. That evening Karen made some statements and evaluations that turned out to be incredibly true. During the next several months, we contacted her on occasion and soon became good friends. Sandy and I told her of Tara's situation and how we had wanted to help Tara get off the medication she had been taking. Karen suggested that she try some relaxation techniques and massage work with Tara. This seemed to help Tara a great deal. Then one day Karen told us something that stayed implanted in my mind for years to come. We were all having a conversation in Karen's home, and she said, "You know, Tara will someday do something to affect millions of people. I am very sure of this, but just be a little cautious during her teenage years." She said this with great conviction. Sandy and I thought that maybe Tara would be a model or an actress and would influence people in that way. We thought that watching out for her in her teens perhaps meant looking out for drugs. Karen made her remark in 1985, and over the next several years as we saw Tara get more involved in modeling and fashion, a vision would periodically flash in front of my eyes as well as Sandy's. We kept seeing Tara's name on a storefront and in cursive writing on a sign or a shopping bag. We didn't know why this vision appeared so many times, but we both experienced it. Of course we saw only the positive in this vision.

Reflecting back on it now, it seems so odd that both Sandy and I had the same vision for so many years. My theory is that before we enter life on this planet, we make an agreement about what our purpose or mission is, and we choose the lessons we need to learn and the people we need to learn them with. And from time to time the veil of "amnesia" is lifted, for only a moment, and we can see what is to be. However, our conscious mind tries to conceal the reality of these thoughts. I do not know where I got this idea; I just know that it feels right.

As the next few years went by, we did all the typical family things, such as taking wonderful vacations and short excursions. All the holidays were special with the four of us. We even managed to appear on a television game show together. It was 1985, and as a family we used to watch *Name That Tune,* which was on in the evenings. I loved playing the game, and with my knowl-edge of music I did quite well from the couch. Sandy encouraged me to try out for the show. I took the initial test and passed and then passed through the interview screening. I was chosen to appear on the show. The show was taped with my three "girls" watching from the audience. There were three rounds to the game, and I managed to score more points, which enabled me to go to the solo round for the big prize and a chance to return for a future championship game. I named all seven tunes in less than thirty seconds. As the bells and buzzers sounded off, Sandy, Tara, and Deanna all came running up on stage to hug me in front of the whole nation. I was now eligible to return to the semi-finals in two weeks. I won the semi-finals, again allowing Sandy, Tara, and Deanna to run on the stage. Then came the finals, for $100,000 in cash and prizes. I never had any dreams of winning; I was just having fun playing. My opponent and I were in the final fifteen seconds of the game, and it occurred to me that I could win. I did! This sent a flood of balloons and streamers falling to the stage, nearly burying my family as they came to cheer me. The four of us couldn't have been any happier.

Sandy and I would often say about our family, "This is what life is all about; nothing else matters." When

Tara reached the age of thirteen, she was like any other teenager—difficult. However, we always felt that Tara had something she was trying to teach us and that there was a reason she was our daughter and we were her parents. Then, when Tara became a freshman in high school (she was about fourteen and three months), she seemed to become more manageable and more mellow. There seemed to be a new energy or softness about her. From a very young age, Tara always looked for the good in people and never judged people based on surface values. She always favored the underdog and could not understand any kind of cruelty that she witnessed. If she saw people begging for money, she would always want to stop and give them something. She wanted to help and give out of pure unconditional love. If Sandy or I were having a conversation with Tara, she would always end it with "I love you," even if we'd been having a heated argument. She wanted to make things right.

3

A New Plane of Existence

We may never be prepared for the road we must travel,
but we can place our trust in God
that wherever it leads
is for our highest good.

In 1988 Sandy and I felt the urge to move fifty miles south to Orange County. We bought a big, beautiful house and Sandy left her current job since I was now able to support the family on my own. Shortly after this, my job was phased out, and we suffered a deep depression due to the severe financial strain. At the time, I felt that our decision to relocate was not the best choice given the outcome, but later I would realize that had we not moved to Orange County, we would not have been in the right place for certain events to occur that were part of our destiny. Our life was right on track in the larger scheme of things.

Through our severe financial hardship, the one thought that Sandy and I held on to was that no matter what happened financially, we still had our family and no one could take that away from us. After several months of not obtaining jobs, we decided to sell our house, as our savings were quickly dwindling away. The first few months went by without any offers and our bank account was empty. I took some odd jobs, and Sandy began looking for substitute teaching jobs. I managed to swallow my pride and ask my estranged father for some money. I had never needed to borrow anything from anyone before, so this was a new experience for me. I realized that my self-esteem was slowly dissolving away, and I couldn't seem to change my situation no matter how hard I tried. I was desperate to move on with my life.

At this difficult time, we found a spiritual belief system that seemed to help and support us through this time and prepare us for the rest of our life. We became very involved in our church and its teachings, and both Tara and Deanna were developing a strong spiritual base. We attended church regularly, believing in our strength and the power of God and realizing that the choices we make in our lives have consequences and they relate directly to our experiences. We discovered that through this time our children were able to learn the importance of love and people and not place much value on material things. Out of every tragedy, a blessing can emerge.

When we were able to come to terms with our situation and understand the reason behind it, things began to change. The house finally sold, and both Sandy and I became gainfully employed. I realized that when we had moved into the upper class neighborhood, subconsciously I had been feeling undeserving and unworthy of the beautiful house and our new lifestyle. I was feeling as if I didn't belong or didn't match up to the caliber of people living in the neighborhood. I was lacking in self-worth. Because of this, I subconsciously created the experience of losing what I had attained. This lesson about how we create the situations in our life would serve as a tool for facing all my other experiences and would help me to cope with each event. I thank God that I was led to a wonderful church and its teachings, or I don't think I could have made it through the rest of my life.

During this time, Tara became extremely spiritual and would discuss her philosophies with her friends and try to help them overcome any obstacles. One day in January 1992, Tara and Sandy were in the church bookstore when Tara discovered a book entitled *Messengers of Light,* by Terry Lynn Taylor. There was a beautiful, ethereal angel on the cover. Tara was drawn to it immediately. As Sandy was talking to the minister, Tara excitedly carried the book up to Sandy and said, "Mom, you have to buy me this book; I really need this book." Tara was not usually quite so insistent about wanting things, but she had a reason for wanting this book so desperately. So Sandy purchased it for her. From that point on, Tara held that book as her prize possession.

Messengers of Light was about reaching out to your angels, communicating with them, learning to listen to them, and responding to them. It served as Tara's connection with the angelic realm. This book enabled her to be open to the possibilities of angelic beings. Tara had discovered a strong and passionate belief system that seemed to be guiding her on her path. During the next several months, she shared the ideas contained in this book with her many friends. She would write notes in it and ask questions that she wanted answered by her angels. I know that somehow she was communicating with her angels. I had a strong feeling that while she was sleeping at night the angels were giving Tara messages and guiding her in some way. I felt as if the angels were beckoning her. In my mind, I could see an angel at the foot of her bed with its arms reaching out and calling to her. I sensed that this was creating an inner conflict in Tara. It was as if she were needed elsewhere to do something important, and she knew the impact her work could have, but it pained her to have to leave a family that was so important to her in order to accomplish this mission. She was only aware of this on a subconscious level, and her destiny was left in God's hands. This strong vision kept repeating itself in my mind.

At this point, I observed Tara undergoing a struggle relating to things and people on a physical plane with her newfound understanding of spirituality and angelic beings. She couldn't understand why conflicts would arise among friends at school and why there couldn't just be pure love and understanding for everyone.

In June 1992, I began to feel a strong sense that some great change was going to occur. I remember sharing with Sandy that I knew our life was on the edge of something new; I had an inner knowing of some impending change that was going to alter our lives forever. With this feeling of anxiousness and uncertainty, I felt the urge to seek a new employer, almost as if I were supposed to be somewhere else. This feeling stayed with me at all times. Soon I started working for a new company, which allowed me some free time and temporarily lessened my stressful workload.

During the past several months, Tara had become very calm and comfortable with herself and seemed to have a clear sense of her identity. In August 1992, Sandy and I took Tara and her best friend, Jen, to Hawaii. With teenagers, parents are never quite sure what to expect, but we had the most perfect vacation that we could ever want. Tara was fun and loving, and she was excited to be spending time with her family and Jen.

One day in Kauai we went shopping, and Tara happened to find some tarot cards that she insisted we buy. We thought it might be fun to experiment with the cards that evening, so Sandy and I sat down with the cards and began to read the instructions. Tara and her friend lost interest before we even began to deal the cards. Sandy dealt my cards first. *Every* card that I was dealt indicated change, devastation, sadness, new beginnings, and loss. Well, I did not find this fun at all—not that I ascribed much validity to the cards. So I quickly shuffled the deck and dealt the cards to Sandy. Strangely enough, the same message came up for Sandy. We quickly put the cards back in the box and sarcastically told Tara, "Thanks a lot!" We went on with the rest of our vacation and had a wonderful time. Running, laughing, and playing on the beaches of Kauai and having wonderful dinners during picturesque sunsets—it was almost too perfect for anyone to believe. My only two regrets were that Deanna wasn't there to share this with us and that it couldn't go on forever.

A New Plane of Existence

When we returned home in early August, Tara, Deanna, and Sandy immediately left for a church teen camp in the mountains. Tara was not feeling herself on the bus ride to the camp and rode the entire trip with her head resting on Sandy's lap. When they arrived, Tara stayed in her cabin alone and began to make three little ceramic angels, one for each member of her family. One had a tear in its eye, which to this day I still find striking. It was very unusual for Tara to spend this much time alone. She was usually such a social butterfly and loved being surrounded by friends. The kids at camp started calling Tara "the angel girl" because of her interest in making angels.

After Tara was feeling better, Sandy remembers Tara saying, "I really want to thank you for taking such good care of me." She said this in such a sincere and loving way that Sandy was deeply touched and at the same time puzzled; it seemed very odd for Tara to say something like that. When they arrived home on August 15, Tara presented each of us with one of her angels. Later on, while Tara was alone with Deanna, she gave her the copy of her beloved book, *Messengers of Light,* even though it was dog-eared and tattered from its many readings. She said, "Deanna, I will always be your guardian angel!"

Deanna was delighted because she knew how important this book was to Tara. Tara also told Deanna, as she pointed to three spots on her stomach, "Deanna, these spots mean eternity; I'll always be with you."

The next day, August 16, Sandy was to drive Deanna to a soccer game about sixty miles away. Tara did not want Sandy to leave and expressed anger about the two of them going. As Sandy was leaving the house, Tara grabbed her arm in such a way and with such strength that it hurt. Tara said in a desperate, demanding tone, "Mom, don't go; don't you ever leave me....Please!" Sandy was very taken back by this request. Tara often spent time with her friends while we were out. At fifteen, children often prefer to be with their peers rather than their parents. Sandy felt bad having to leave, but she reminded Tara that I would be home soon. When I arrived home, Tara seemed to be deep in thought and was feeling very alone. She wanted to talk and didn't like the idea that I was preoccupied with rushing to get to Deanna's soccer game. She begged me not to leave, which again was uncommon. I then asked her if she would like to drive out to the field with me and watch the game. I didn't expect Tara would come because she did not enjoy sports much and would usually choose to socialize with her own friends rather than attend a soccer game. To my surprise and delight, Tara accepted.

I now thank God and the angels for that one and a half-hour drive with Tara. The two of us talked about plans for her future and what she really wanted in her life. She often felt that she hadn't made her mark or accomplished anything of importance, whereas Deanna had her sports involvement. Tara enjoyed fashion and modeling, so we discussed getting some photos taken so she could pursue something related to modeling. I will never forget the look on her face as I said this. She turned to me with her beautiful smile and her eyes glowing and responded, "Do you really mean that? I would love it!" The scene with her smiling and turning toward me would play over and over again in my mind for years to come. I felt that we had closure on so many things that day. Why had Tara accepted my invitation to the soccer game? Why did I feel such a sense of closure and peace? Why was I feeling so complete and whole as a father?

We arrived at the field, and it was extremely hot—in the high nineties. Everyone was complaining about the heat, but not Tara. She was watching Deanna's game with excitement and joy, and she appeared so content—unlike the other spectators. There was a difference about her, a completeness and a beauty I had not seen previously. I can still see her cheering for her sister and rooting for the team. How proud I was of both my daughters. This was a wonderful day! This was a wonderful life!

On August 17, Tara had a dentist appointment. I remember how lethargic she seemed that day. I got the impression she was just drifting through the day. She was wearing ugly cowboy boots that didn't really complement the rest of her outfit, but she still looked like an angel. She was having a root canal completed at the dentist—her first. She didn't complain of any pain and just continued with her day as though nothing out of the ordinary had happened. The four of us had dinner that night and played a family game. It got late, and we were all tired, so I tucked Deanna into bed, said good night, and hugged her. I went into Tara's room and said good night and told her I loved her. Tara responded with, "I love you too, Daddy." That was the last time I saw her and the last words I would hear her say.

The next morning, I got up early to go to work, careful not to wake anyone. I had a very busy day scheduled. I had a last-minute appointment arranged at 6:30 P.M., and I was to accompany the church choir at 7:30 P.M. While I was at choir, Sandy was home with Tara and two of her girlfriends and Deanna and her girlfriend. Tara was making dinner for everyone and had also made a birthday cake for her boyfriend, who was returning home from a vacation that evening. She was laughing and making jokes all evening. It was obvious that Tara was at her best, her pinnacle. Then suddenly at dinner the conversation and laughing stopped, and there was an eerie silence. As a serious expression came over Tara's face, she asked Sandy a very haunting question. She looked into Sandy's eyes and said, "Mom, do you feel that when you have completed your work on this plane of existence that you can go at any time to do something more meaningful on another plane of existence?" There was a moment of silence as a piercing gaze occurred between them and the other girls looked on. Then Sandy responded, "Of course, Tara, you know I believe that is a possibility." With that having been said, all the girls continued their evening of fun. Sandy observed the joy in the house that night and thought, "This is what life is all about—being with your family and laughing and sharing the love and joy that children bring." But Tara's comment still puzzled Sandy.

At about 8:30 P.M. one of the girls had to return to her home. Tara's friend, who was sixteen, said she would be glad to drive her home. Tara said, "Great, I'll go with you. Bye, Mom. We'll be back in a few minutes. I love you."

At about 9:30, I was nearing home. I began to drive up the hill entering our neighborhood, but the road was blocked off. There were barricades surrounded by flares. There were ambulances and firetrucks and people surrounding this chaos. What a sight! I had a pit in my stomach and immediately turned around and headed for the back entrance to our home. When I walked in, I saw Sandy, Deanna, and her friend watching television. I said to Sandy, "I'm sorry about being late, but there was a terrible accident on the street up the hill and the road was blocked off." Sandy immediately grew pale, her joyful face becoming panic-stricken. She said in a frantic voice, "Oh my God! It's Tara. We must go."

I pushed any thought of Tara having an accident right out of my mind. We sent Deanna and her friend to a neighbor's house and drove down to the site of the accident. People were milling around, wondering what had happened. We made our way through the barricade, trying to observe the scene. One hundred yards away, Sandy spotted the vehicle. "Oh no!" Sandy said. "That's their car—oh my God!" Sandy became engulfed in feelings of despair and pain. It was the car that belonged to Tara's friend. People were trying to find out what had happened, while I held Sandy together and attempted to get some answers. One person was saying that there had been three girls in the car; two were fine, and the other had died. Others were saying they were all fine. Finally we made our way to a policeman and asked him for some information. He said the girls had been taken to the hospital and that we would have to go there to obtain any information.

As our neighbors drove us to the hospital, I was still unsure what to expect. My head was swimming, but I was holding on to positive thoughts, as I believed that nothing terrible could ever happen to us—not with the beautiful life we had created over the many years we had been a family unit. We arrived at the hospital and dashed to the emergency room. I walked up to the main desk and explained that my daughter had been taken there after a bad car accident. The nurses immediately began asking me to fill out forms and to tell them about my insurance coverage. I couldn't think, and I finally said, "Just tell me how my daughter is—*now, please.*"

The nurses ushered Sandy and me into a waiting room filled with people we did not know. I remember thinking, "Who are these people? Why are they here? I need to know what's going on." We then realized that among these many strangers were the parents of the other two girls. Then a nurse entered the room full of people and asked who the parents of the first girl were. They identified themselves, and the nurse said their daughter was fine. Then the parents of the second girl were asked to identify themselves, and the nurse said she was doing fine. Then the nurse asked for the parents of Tara Moore. My heart froze. I felt as if I were watching a movie; this

43

could not be my life. The nurse said without a flinch, "Tara didn't make it." In a room full of people we did not know, with no respect for our feelings, the nurse made this statement. Sandy became hysterical and was unable to calm herself. Our worst nightmare had happened. I tried to convince myself that I hadn't heard these words. This couldn't possibly be happening. I attempted to hold on to Sandy as I tried to put my feelings of devastation and disbelief aside. I screamed at the nurse to get Sandy a tranquilizer or sedative—to do something to calm her. I couldn't believe where I was and what I was witnessing. I was wrenched with pain as I watched Sandy out of control. Nobody was doing anything to help.

Sandy ran toward the exit of the hospital, and I ran after her in an attempt to comfort her. We paced up and down the sidewalk in front of the hospital, both of us muttering that we could not believe this was happening. How could God allow this to happen? What was the purpose in all this? My head was spinning. All I could think of now was getting home and telling Deanna what had occurred. I just wanted us to be with Deanna. "Oh my God! How is Deanna going to deal with this? She and Tara were best friends. Oh, this can't be happening!"

We pulled up in front of our house, only to observe a group of neighbors and friends surrounding our driveway, all waiting to help and support us. Deanna was standing out front. As I got out of the car, I called for Deanna and said, "Please come here. I need to talk to you." Before I could even tell her what had happened, Deanna started walking away from me, displaying a look of disbelief. Somehow she knew but didn't want to believe. As I tried to approach her, she began to cry out, "No! No! I know Tara is okay. No! I don't want to talk to you." She began to move faster and faster and kept saying, "I know Tara's okay. I know she is." I was able to grab Deanna and cling onto her and carry her into the house. We sat on the sofa, and I told her what had happened. Deanna burst into tears, and I could feel her emotions and her life being ripped apart. I felt her having to mature in that one instant because her life had changed forever and nothing would ever be the same. As a man, as a father, I had always tried to protect my children from anything unpleasant. I had always been in control of making sure they had what they needed. Now all the rules had changed; I had no control, and I couldn't change these events or protect my family from this devastation. There was nothing I could say or do to fix this. That night I not only lost one daugher, but two. I couldn't bear to see the pain that both Sandy and Deanna had to endure.

Through her tears, Deanna began sharing with Sandy and me that this wasn't the way things were supposed to be. She told us of all the plans that she and Tara had for the rest of their lives. She said that Tara was going to get married someday and that they would buy two houses next to each other—one for her and one for Deanna— so that they would always be there for whatever they needed, whether a cup of sugar or just a hug. They had always talked of supporting each other and being best friends. They had planned to live the rest of their lives inseparable. I saw Deanna's dreams being shattered, and all I could do was hold her in my arms. I just wanted to remain frozen in this moment and not have to do anything else the rest of my life. But there had to be a reason.

4

Accepting Reality With Love and Understanding

The sorrows we experience in life
allow our heart to stretch
and make room for even greater love.
Embrace the difficulties and learn from them.

By midnight everyone had left, and as the three of us sat alone we could feel the dark, the quiet, the emptiness, and most of all the unknown. We sank into the loneliness and decided to light a candle and say a prayer to Tara, sending her love and peace, knowing she was in God's hands. We wondered if the angels had been calling for Tara to do some work that was more important on the other side. I kept seeing a mental picture of an angel motioning to Tara to join them, telling her she was needed to do some intense work. It was as if Tara were being sucked up into a vacuum, with little resistance on her part. But how could she leave us with such devastation? How could she leave a family that loved her so much? What could be more important than remaining with her family? Was there perhaps a greater plan for all of us? I knew there had to be some reason for this experience, but I felt too much sadness at this point to be clear, and only with time would this puzzle piece fit into place and begin to make sense.

We heard a knock at the door, and it was Tara's boyfriend, Brian, with his parents. He had just arrived home, and they had heard the news of Tara's death. He came into our house and could not hold back his sadness. We all hugged and cried and shared our disbelief. Then we took Brian into the kitchen and showed him the birthday cake Tara had made: "HAPPY BIRTHDAY, BRIAN." It was too much for him to handle. Brian, like the rest of us, was in shock and not ready to deal with the situation.

Soon after Brian and his family left, Sandy and I went into the kitchen to put the cake away. Just then, I looked on the kitchen counter, and to my amazement I found one angel-shaped cookie all by itself. We asked one another, knowing that Tara must have made it, where she had gotten the dough and the cookie cutter and when she could have made it. This was extremely puzzling, but then the whole evening had been a mass of confusion. We decided to try and get some sleep. After a few hours, I awoke, wondering if all the events of the preceding evening had been a dream. It was all too unreal and did not even seem possible. The mind has an interesting way of protecting us when we need it most. Although I knew that Tara's death was real, I was in shock, which cushioned me from the reality so the pain would not be as intense. I got out of bed and walked by Tara's bedroom, opened the door, and noticed something on the floor of her room. I called to Sandy so I could show her what I had found. It was the words to a single song torn out of a songbook entitled "You're an Angel."

*You're an Angel**

You're an angel, you're a being of light.
You're an angel, and I know that I'm right.
You're an angel, bringing love to everyone.
And it's yours to give,
And in the giving comes the fun.

We are angels, we are beings of light.
We are angels, and we know that we're right.
We are angels, bringing love to everyone.
And it's ours to give,
And in the giving comes the fun.

I'm an angel, I'm a being of light.
I'm an angel, and I know that I'm right.
I'm an angel, bringing love to everyone.
And it's mine to give,
And in the giving comes the fun.

---

*You're an Angel" by Charley Thweatt is used with permission. Copyright © 1983 Angelight Music.

With all the signs that had appeared, we knew there was a message that Tara was trying to convey to us. She was an angel. The angels had been calling for her soul. My vision of the angels beckoning to Tara to leave for something more important was true. The signs that she had left and would continue to leave were laying out a path that we had to follow in order for us to discover our purpose and mission in this lifetime. Once our minds were clear, we would eventually get the message that was trying to make itself known.

The next day, it was very important to us that we visit the hospital and see the other two girls who had been in the vehicle. Physically they were fine, but we wanted to make sure that emotionally they would heal and feel no responsibility for what had happened. We shared our love with them and told them that it was Tara's time and to try to heal as best they could. Jill, the girl sitting directly behind Tara in the car, shared with us that just before they had driven away last evening, Tara had wanted her to hold one of the ceramic angels she had made at camp. Jill felt in some way that the angel had spared her life. With the comment that Tara had made the preceding night at the dinner table, the girls were wondering if Tara had truly known her own destiny.

The next couple of days were a blur. Multitudes of people were in and out of our house. Flowers arrived in droves, and, interestingly enough, angel statues, cards, and mementos. People said they were inspired to send angels. There were articles in the newspapers, and news reporters from television came to do a story about Tara regarding the accident. I was told they had been flooded with calls from all those who knew Tara. The memorial service was held in our church, which has the capacity to seat 250 people. Five hundred people attended the memorial service—people from all over California. Many of Tara's friends wrote cards, poems, and letters to us explaining how they knew Tara was an angel and how spiritual she had become. I was amazed at how many people Tara's life had touched. I had no idea of the impact that her life and death was having on everyone. One of her very good friends wrote the following letter to Sandy and me, which was read at Tara's memorial service:

Dear Mr. and Mrs. Moore and Deanna,

Tara was a very beautiful, loving spiritual girl. She was my only spiritual friend. She was the only friend I could talk to about my problems, who could help me by using the knowledge of the universe. The time that I spent

51

with her was the most spiritual time in my life, and for that I am grateful. She brought God closer to me and taught me that spirituality isn't something that you just practice at home, but is something that you can carry within you wherever you go. And yet, through all of the things she taught me about spirituality, she saved the most powerful yet painful one for last. She left the precious gift of knowledge, acceptance, and understanding of death.

Tara is now an angelic being surrounded by her spirit guides and guardian angels. Her life has not ended; she has only left the earth realm to visit a different part of the universe. Her soul, her light, will never die. As she travels the universe she will only grow stronger and more enlightened and closer to the divine being. Her soul lives on just as we do and grows just as the universe grows.

Love always...

This letter was written by a fifteen-year-old girl who had become very close to Tara.

At the memorial service, Sandy managed to speak a few words in a loving good-bye to Tara. In a quivering voice, she stated that Tara must have had something very important to do to leave a family that loved her so much and that she loved equally. Sandy spoke of how she supported Tara in her purpose on Earth and now in carrying that purpose to a new dimension. And then, surrounded by all the people who loved Tara, Sandy acknowledged the love that consumed the room that day by saying to Tara, "Tara, there are so many people here who love you and appreciate you. As your mother, I want this to be your sixteenth birthday, your high school graduation, your wedding day. You always loved parties and being social. So with all your friends here today, this is a celebration for you. I love you."

As the service continued, I clung to one thought that our minister had spoken. Her talk revolved around the eternal spirit and the continuation of life even though the human form is not present. She made a very poignant statement that in death we often perceive only the loss of a beautiful soul, giving no thought to the joyous arrival of that soul that is occurring on another plane. Thinking of that transitional aspect of the soul has given me a great deal of peace and comfort. I know it is true.

Because of the severity of the accident, we were never given the option of seeing Tara's body. Since we believe that the spirit never dies and that the body is only a vessel for that spirit, we were able to come to terms with having Tara cremated. Although we had never discussed this topic with Tara, we were sure this is what she would have wanted. Given Tara's love of the beach and the ocean, we decided to spread her ashes at sea. Sandy and I thought that since we had recently been to Hawaii and that vacation had been such a gift, we would buy a beautiful purple (Tara's favorite color) lei instead of other flowers. Sandy, her mother, Deanna, Brian, and I chartered a boat and began our voyage out to sea. We had a musical tape playing "You're an Angel" and "Tara's Theme" from *Gone With the Wind*. Deanna was wearing the lei. When the boat stopped, we scattered the ashes at sea. Deanna removed the lei from around her neck as we all spoke our loving thoughts. We kissed the lei and flung it into the air. It drifted overboard and then landed gently on the water. We stared at it as the rocking waves seemed to embrace it. Then something very magical occurred. The four of us witnessed the lei forming a perfect heart-shaped arrangement. We knew that this incredible sign was Tara's way of saying "I love you, and I will always be with you in spirit." That scene will forever remain vivid in our minds. I know that this was a beautiful message from a new angel.

5

The Message in the Heart as Divine Guidance

*Listen to your heart's intuition,
and follow its guidance.
This is God's message
being passed on to you.*

My life took on a new dimension. When you go through a tragedy like this, your perception of life changes. Everything takes on a new appearance. Nothing means the same as it did before. I knew my life needed to head in a new direction. I attempted to return to my job, but it felt meaningless. What I did no longer mattered. I was no longer able to concentrate on this mundane work, and I felt different from everyone else. There was something greater out there that Sandy and I had to pursue.

With all the angel signs and messages we had been given, we realized that the path was being laid down right in front of us. All we had to do was to be open, listen, and respond to what the universe had in store for us. Again, this was part of the master plan for our mission in life. There are no accidents, just experiences that lead us to the next step of our evolution. I knew that we had been chosen and had agreed at some point in our spiritual evolution to do something that would open people's consciousness. Tara happened to be the catalyst for this experience. We decided to take this negative event and try to turn it into something positive and purposeful.

An idea emerged that seemed so natural we couldn't ignore it. When an idea or thought continually nudges you and you cannot erase or ignore that thought, you have two choices: to be passive about it and cast it aside and not listen or to be open to the possibilities and follow your heart and let your own true divinity chart a course for you that can create a new world. We chose the latter and followed our calling. With all the angelic signs that had surfaced in our life, we knew that opening an angel store was what we had to do. There was no question that this was the message, our calling, our mission.

We had never had our own business nor did we have any retail experience, but that didn't matter. This was more than a business venture; this was an opportunity to get a message out to the world. We were guided and driven to make this happen—to make a statement and make a difference. How we would do this was not important; only our intent in what we were doing mattered. Everything else would take care of itself. When we asked questions about how to do something, these questions were always answered. When we needed guidance about something, the right person would miraculously show up in our lives to help support us and guide us. Everything happened effortlessly and seemed to flow perfectly. We knew that Tara had a message to convey and that we were the vehicles for it. We needed to create hope and inspiration out of such a tragedy. Angels are messengers of God, and they do exist. They are love, joy, and beauty. Their message of hope and inspiration is there to open the hearts and consciousness of all people.

Without Tara in the house, an uncomfortable quietness had begun to dominate. I missed the radio blasting, the sound of feet running up and down the stairs, and all the friends Tara used to have in the house. The stillness, or lack of exhilarating energy, was too difficult to bear. Deanna became withdrawn and pulled into herself. She neglected her friends, her wit and humor had almost vanished, and she lost interest in many things she had once cherished. She was in deep pain and harboring intense anger. She had lost her childlike innocence and the smile that everyone had loved. She hated her life.

Often she would retreat to her room and draw or write poetry for hours, trying to find answers to this experience. None came—only pain and loneliness. She wouldn't express her feelings to us or talk about Tara. Her heart had been penetrated so deeply that no counseling or therapy could aid her in healing—only time.

Not being able to get through to Deanna or help her pained both Sandy and me greatly. Sandy herself was in so much pain that she was grateful just to make it through another day. Actually, Sandy was much stronger than she gave herself credit for. She refused to take any medication because she did not want to be numbed to life. She wanted to experience her grief and sadness. She wanted to express. She returned to teaching in the fall— just three weeks after the accident. She wanted to be strong, and she was. She broke down daily, but that was okay. There is no right or wrong way to grieve. She did the best she could for everyone else. Sandy never wallowed in self-pity or presented herself as a victim. She, too, knew that some souls choose to be here only a brief time and that we have chosen to be part of this experience in this lifetime. However, no matter how spiritual we are, human emotions are important and play a large role in our development.

I was at a loss about what to do. I couldn't fix things or glue them back together. I was unable to help Deanna, or make Sandy happy, or even nurture myself. I was lost and deflated. It took too much effort to get up each morning or go to sleep each night. But I had to, so I did. It became very difficult to remain in the same house and neighborhood. Driving up and down the street where the accident occurred was much too painful, especially since there was a memorial created at the curbside right where the accident happened. Many of Tara's high school friends had created this memorial in her honor. It was their way of showing respect. There was a cross, flowers every day, and notes and letters that were dropped off on a daily basis. Painted in the street in large red letters was the question "WHY HER, GOD?"

We decided to sell our house and get a fresh start in a new neighborhood. The house took just a few months to sell. The night before we moved, it occurred to me that perhaps we were not doing the right thing in moving. I was in the kitchen surrounded by all the packed cartons, and I suddenly began to question our reasons. Were we trying to leave our sorrow behind, or the memories of our happy life with Tara? Were we doing the right thing? I felt for a moment that we *were* leaving Tara behind. And as I looked up into the dark night, I heard a voice immediately say, "Don't worry; you're not leaving me behind. I'll be with you wherever you are." It was Tara's voice I heard, not my mind conjuring up words. I realized that I had most definitely gotten a response. I felt such relief, I was moved to tears. I have never seen an angel, but I have certainly felt an angelic presence and heard the voice of one. From that moment on, I knew Tara's presence would always be with us, even though the physical being no longer existed.

The guidance we received over the next several months in preparing to open the angel store was truly divine. We experienced no fear and no concern—only the knowing that this was the perfect action taking place in our lives. I was once told by someone that when you move forward effortlessly with no obstacles, your direction can only be right. If you happen to meet roadblocks, this most likely means that there is a process you must go through first in order to achieve results.

As the shock of Tara's death began to diminish, it was replaced by sadness and loneliness. We all missed Tara and the life we had known together. I used to go into Tara's room and hold the beautiful black dress that she wore to the Winter Formal. The fragrance of the perfume she always wore still clung to the fabric. Ironically, it was Eternity. Some times I would pretend we were dancing at her wedding. I would talk to her. How could I ever lead a normal existence? I so wanted to experience a physical visitation from Tara, but I realized that it would probably be too painful to see her.

I have always been a person who experiences a lot through my dreams, and I have received many messages while in the sleeping state. For me, this is when I am most receptive and open to what the universe is saying to me. I remember Tara coming to me one night in a vivid dream. Sandy, Deanna, and I were in a very dark room, and we couldn't see anything except a small round hole above us. An intense light was shining through the hole. I was struggling to get us up through the hole into the light, and it seemed almost impossible. Finally, we made it to the other side. There, in amazement, I looked around. I was in awe at the beauty. The light was so much brighter than sunlight. A vibrant blue shoreline nestled up to a grassy area, where each blade of grass appeared to be electrified with the color green. Mountains rose just beyond the grass. It was as if all of nature had met in one beautiful scene. The sky was a pale blue, with a slight calming breeze. The peacefulness of this encounter caused me to feel euphoric and tranquil and very much at home. With Sandy and Deanna at my side, I suddenly noticed a radiant being dressed in white moving toward us. It was Tara, her hair blowing gently in the breeze. She had a loving smile as she approached us, and

I could feel such immense love pouring out of her. I remember the three of us standing close together while Tara stood a few feet away. There was no physical contact, just a feeling of love, acceptance, and understanding. She spoke to us of joy and contentment. Then beautiful music surrounded her as the conversation ended.

When I awoke the next morning, I realized that this was a comfortable way for Tara to communicate with me, although it made me miss her all the more. I analyzed my experience and was able to determine what it all meant. The three of us in the dark represented our sadness, and the light on the other side was Tara's new home. The beauty there was heaven, the spirit world, the place where angels live. It was a miraculous place where the feelings of love and joy permeate your entire being. I got a glimpse of this perfect world for an instant. The separation of the three of us and Tara let me know that although we are in different worlds, communication still exists and love never dies—it just changes form. I realized that while my mind was at rest and in a subconscious state, I had the ability to receive messages and I could let this communication help guide me on my path. On a more casual level, this might be considered intuition. But what I had experienced was much more powerful.

In preparing to open the store, the only detail that Sandy and I could not get clear on was the location. We looked at several available spaces, but nothing felt right. We finally asked for some guidance in this area and left it in the hands of the universe. Then one night while I was sleeping, another message came to me. In this dream or vision, I saw a place called the Franciscan Plaza in San Juan Capistrano. That is all I remember about the dream. It was very evident that I was being told about this plaza in my dream. Sandy and I had driven by it a few times but had never visited it. We really didn't know anything about it. In fact, we had never considered San Juan Capistrano as a potential site for the store.

The next day I told Sandy about my dream, and we decided to see what this plaza had to offer. It was an extremely quaint little plaza with about fifteen shops. It had abundant charm, but there were no spaces available except one tiny little shop hidden in a corner on the lowest level. We walked up to the space with its windows all covered in paper so no one could look in. The sign on the door said that 350 square feet were available. We looked at each other and discussed the size. Although we couldn't see inside, 350 square feet seemed too small based on our plans for a store with a minimum of 700 square feet. We left the plaza with some disappointment because the surroundings felt so right, and we began thinking that if we used the 350 square feet creatively, maybe it would work. A smaller store would also make our rent payments much lower. We decided it could work out, and the location could not have been more perfect. I know the angels were communicating to me in my dreams to seek out this location. This area is filled with tourists and is very accessible. It is just one block south of Mission San Juan Capistrano, and the angels knew that this was a place that people from many parts of the country would visit. We would be in the right place to make a difference.

We decided to approach the landlord to see about renting the space for the angel store. We were hopeful that he would be receptive to our idea. We were two people who have never owned a business wanting to open a store dedicated totally to angels. I remember Sandy saying, "God, please, just let him keep an open mind."

I was unable to meet with the landlord due to my schedule, so Sandy and Deanna approached him the next day after setting an appointment with him over the telephone. The first words out of his mouth when they told him our idea were, "An angel store? I promise I will keep an open mind while you explain." He did keep an open mind, although I know he was skeptical. He asked us to submit a business plan and to look over the lease. We followed his instructions, and I returned the items the very next day. One thing I asked for in the lease was that when a more desirable location became available, we would be offered the first option on that location. I had my eye on the storefront that currently housed a T-shirt shop. It was the best location in the plaza and the most visible. I told the landlord that someday we were going to be a landmark, and we needed the best space we could get. He smiled at me, and I'm sure he thought I was all talk. But I knew that every word I spoke was the truth, and I had my sights set on something bigger than the tiny space that was currently available. We eventually came to terms and began preparations for opening the store.

As we got ready to open the store, Sandy and I tried to include Deanna in our venture whenever possible. Sandy and I felt that we were being divinely guided through this whole phase of opening the store, and it was evident that our minds were preoccupied and we didn't have a lot of time to be sad over our loss. I was concerned about Deanna and felt her loneliness. Sandy and I had each other, but Deanna had no one. Because I was so concerned with this, I experienced another dream, visitation, or vision. I dreamt that I was observing a beautiful scene in a meadow on a sunny afternoon. I was not part of the scene but just an observer. I saw Deanna standing in the meadow as if she were waiting for someone, and then I witnessed Tara running up to her and throwing her arms around her, giving her the biggest hug and smile I had ever seen. I could both see and feel an overwhelming sensation of love and peace. The two of them sat talking, laughing, and loving for the longest time. I remember the absolute joy I felt while watching this reunion.

Deanna was not very open about her feelings, and I was hesitant at times to share thoughts of Tara with her. About one week after my dream about their reunion, we were all having dinner, and Deanna appeared to be in an open frame of mind and eager to share. So I asked her if she ever had dreams of Tara. She then shared with us that about a week ago she had dreamt that she and Tara were in a meadow hugging and laughing and talking about fun things. She said she could feel Tara's love so strongly in that moment. My eyes welled up with tears as I knew Tara had connected all our thoughts that one night so we could experience the love she wanted to communicate.

Dreams seemed to be my clearest source for communicating with and receiving messages from the angelic realm. But this process required me to be open and willing to receive what I needed.

6

The Pieces of the Puzzle
Start to Come Together

When we are divinely connected,
we become co-creators with God,
creating a path in life that allows us
to fulfill our highest purpose.

On September 10, 1993, Tara's Angels opened its doors. As the sign in cursive writing was being hung over the door, Sandy and I looked at the shop filled with angels and cried as we realized this was just what we had foreseen several years ago. We wondered how this had all come about, how we had managed to pull all this together. We truly felt as though we were the vehicles of a higher power. Something greater than ourselves was at work here. Customers began visiting the store. Many stated that they were somehow guided here, and many, upon entering, said they definitely felt an angelic presence. Some said they felt the presence of eleven angels. On the front counter, we made available a pamphlet entitled "The Story of Tara's Angels," which gave a brief history of how the store came into being through our tragic loss and the love of angels that Tara had left with us. People would come into the store and cry, sharing their feelings and perhaps a loss that they had experienced. We were told several times a day that there was a comfort in being in the store and that people felt safe sharing with us.

Tara's Angels was not just a retail shop; it was more. We were living our purpose. We knew that! The store was a mission we were meant to carry out—part of a plan, the reason we were here. I recalled knowing as a child that someday I would have my own business; this had always been a desire of mine. My dream or vision or plan was real. I was doing what the angels had foretold. I would soon discover that this was a major piece of the jigsaw puzzle.

Soon after we opened, the attention we received from the media was uncanny. Tara had always wanted to be famous: a model, an actress, or a speaker. She wanted to make a difference. We were contacted by a local newspaper, *The Capistrano Valley News,* which wanted to do an article on the store and the story behind it. This attracted many local residents to the store. Then the

Orange County Register heard about it. They did an even more elaborate story in their business section. This brought even more people to the store. Then the *Los Angeles Times* wanted to do a front-page story, and we couldn't keep people away. We knew that Tara was having fun orchestrating all these events to get her name and the angels out there for everyone.

As the store gradually became well known, I still kept my other job in order to ensure an income for the three of us. I found it very difficult to juggle the two, especially since my passion was being part of Tara's Angels. But it was necessary at this stage of the business. Sandy, Deanna, and I continued therapy in dealing with the loss of Tara. We were still grieving heavily from this devastating experience. We constantly asked our angels for help and guidance in making it through each day. It was still an effort. The first thought each morning upon waking and the last thought before going to sleep each night was the loss of our beloved Tara. We somehow found the strength each day to get out of bed and get on with our lives.

Trying to heal this major wound was a difficult task, and we would often ask ourselves what the purpose in all of this was. We felt that every lesson in life had a purpose. It is often said that God does not give us more than we can handle, although sometimes the burden does feel overwhelming. We kept our faith. We found ourselves supported and nurtured by our good friends. Sandy and I did the best we could to nurture each other and Deanna.

One day a very good friend recommended that I might try counseling with a hypnotherapist. My friend had just completed a session and suggested I contact Marillyn Brame, a woman with outstanding credentials. I set up an appointment and anxiously awaited my first visit. I had never been hypnotized and did not know what to expect. At the first session, she explained to me what her method was and what she wanted to accomplish. She used a method called the time line. Once I was hypnotized, she would have me visualize a time line extending in space. She then would ask me to float over this time line and focus on some period in my life that I needed to understand better. More than anything, I wanted to know my purpose in life, why I had experienced the loss of a child, and how I could make sense of the confusion I felt. We completed the first session, and I was amazed at the process. Being hypnotized was so different from what I had expected. I was extremely aware of everything I was saying and feeling. Marillyn had taken me back to some childhood experiences, and it was more than just recall; I actually felt the feelings I had had at that time. Many times during the session, I cried and felt deep sadness without control of the emotion. I could see things and remember things that I couldn't have recalled in a conscious state of mind, but they were all clear when I returned to normal consciousness. I was so impressed that I scheduled a second appointment.

At my second appointment, I learned something that helped me make sense of my whole being, my purpose, and why I was here. This was to be part of the answer that I was searching for, but it would lead to other questions.

I went into this session more relaxed than the first because I knew what to expect. I quickly entered a trance as Marillyn talked me through a peaceful setting. We once again visited my time line. This time I went back to 1961. I was hovering over my body as it lay on the ground after my fall. There I was, watching that scene that had played over and over again in my mind so many times. Marillyn asked me what I saw, which I easily described to her, but as I was speaking I was flooded with tears. I was feeling my mother's pain when she thought I was dead. Then, through my tears, I asked the therapist a question: "Why did I live? Why didn't I die?" Then something occurred that was so awesome and overwhelming I couldn't speak. Marillyn took me a little deeper and asked me what I saw. I couldn't believe what I was witnessing. I was standing in front of three very large angels who were emitting a very bright and powerful white light. All I could see was their form, and one was

71

larger than the other two. There were no distinct characteristics except for their form and the wonderful light. I was speaking to them, and they were responding. I then asked a question that would help me to understand what my life was all about and why I had chosen to come back—another piece of the puzzle.

As I stood before these three beings, I asked them desperately why I came back to life. This question seemed so important that the rest of my life seemed to depend on the response. I had an overwhelming feeling, as if I were speaking to royalty, although I know now that these higher beings, these angels, were about to give me a message. I was feeling anxious as their message came forth. Their answer was not spoken, but rather conveyed directly to my inner being. It is very difficult to describe, as it is not a means of communication that occurs in our normal conscious state. When I asked, "Why did I live?" their communication began with, "You have been chosen." I remember wondering, "Chosen for what?" They responded, "You have been chosen for a mission. You have a purpose."

Although this experience had occurred nearly thirty-three years before, my subconscious was now remembering each detail as if no time had passed. Marillyn continued to lead me through this experience while taking notes and asking questions. I then asked the angels,

"When will I know what this purpose or mission is?" Their response was not a surprise to me, nor did it satisfy my curiosity. In a comforting and supportive manner, they responded, "Soon." I have discovered that in the spirit world, there is no concept of time. "Soon" can mean thirty minutes or thirty years. So I accepted their response, knowing that I would discover my purpose and mission when I was supposed to discover it. I somehow knew that there was something else that had occurred while I was unconscious, but at this time I was unable to recall it, or maybe I was just too overwhelmed by the events that had taken place.

Tears were now streaming down my face, and Marillyn could feel my awe and sadness at leaving the angels as she pulled me back to the present. She then said that she would like to take me, subconsciously, into the future through her time line method. I could sense that she felt this might help me deal with my grief. Her plan was to take me to the end of my life here on Earth as I made my transition into the next existence. Of course, who was there to greet me with a great big smile but Tara! She was pure beauty and love (two of the most angelic qualities). She was so excited to see me that she grabbed my arm and started leading me in the right direction. She was talking incessantly and telling me how the angel store was the best idea and the most wonderful thing that we could ever have done. She was commenting on how successful it was and how proud she was of us for doing such a brave thing. My eyes welled up with tears. She continued her expression of love and joy as she escorted me on a timeless journey through the universe. I felt so complete and filled with purpose. I was truly saddened when this episode came to a close. I felt as though I wanted to remain in this dimension indefinitely, but there was much more work for me to do.

Marillyn allowed me time to compose myself before speaking. She appeared to be in awe of my journey. We discussed the events and then ended this miraculous session.

With the Christmas season upon us and all the exposure from the press we had received, the store was unbelievably busy. Most of the time it was difficult to shop in the store because of the crowds of customers. We had planned a trip to Costa Rica leaving Christmas Day in order to rest up from the long hours and heavy workload of the store. We also found some solace in "escaping" during the holidays (especially Christmas), so as not to feel the sadness and loneliness of experiencing this special time of year without Tara. The vacation to Costa Rica, however, ended up being very disappointing. I feel that we all create our own experience, and this vacation, or adventure as I like to refer to it, was indicative of my life at the time.

We planned to stay at three different places while in Costa Rica because our travel agent had recommended we visit at least three locations to get a true overview of the country. Once the plane landed, we quickly rented a four-wheel-drive jeep and headed for our first destination. I had no idea how primitive and undeveloped Costa Rica was. Nor was I aware of how much driving I would have to do in order to reach our destination. The endless driving over potholed, single-laned roads was more exhausting than I had expected. We had to travel over questionable-looking suspension bridges and gravel roads that created such a haze of dust I could barely see. Hordes of cows often crossed the road, causing many delays. Every time I drove up to another obstacle, another detour, I felt like Indiana Jones on one of his many adventures. Getting from point A to point B was a real challenge. Every time we made it over one hurdle and thought we were home free, another roadblock presented itself. I found myself dealing with anger, frustration, and constant agitation. I realized that this experience was mirroring my thoughts and my life. Dealing with the loss of Tara and our changing family dynamics was also a journey from one point to the next—sometimes smooth, but often bumpy. The emotional roadblocks that kept popping up created a delay in my journey, but determination would keep me going. There was a final destination to reach, but the challenge was the process of getting there. The challenge was crossing each bridge and landing in a safe place, but it was a long journey, a long road—much more traveling than I had expected. I just wanted to go home where I could feel some sense of comfort. That's interesting—going home, feeling comfort. What was that?

I realized that our expectations of getting away by going to Costa Rica were not being met. Although we could escape the hectic pace of the shop, we couldn't escape our thoughts or what was in our hearts. I hadn't been confronting my life, or what was left of it. I had immersed myself in work and did not want to face my deeper feelings. Anger and resentment had been building up inside and needed to be acknowledged. No matter how spiritual our perspective, human emotions demand our attention at times. Healing would involve an ongoing process of emotional catharsis and reminders of a spiritual perspective.

We returned from our vacation in January and quickly reestablished our normal routine. Shortly after our return, we received a telephone call that would result in a life-altering experience and the next catalyst of my journey, Sandy's journey, and Deanna's journey.

It was a very quiet day in the store as the rain pounded on the roof. There were no customers, and the sound of the rain against the silence of the room was relaxing. The sound of the phone ringing broke the stillness and brought me back to the present. It was a call from a man associated with an independent film company who was making an angel documentary. He had gotten our name from Terry Lynn Taylor, who had heard of our store and our angel experience regarding Tara. Terry Lynn Taylor knew the important role her book *Messengers of Light* had played in Tara's life. The man, Rex, explained that they wanted to make a documentary on angels for home video use that would include various people's angel experiences. He stated that he wanted to do some filming in our store and then interview us at our home. We agreed to meet with him and his crew with the understanding that our story would be covered with integrity. We did not want it sensationalized or exploited in any way. We wanted it to be credible and done in a tasteful manner. Rex assured me that he held the same vision. Sandy and I knew that once again Tara was coordinating this event and handpicking the people she wanted involved. This was another avenue for her to get her message out, and again we were the vehicles—another part of our mission.

When Rex and his crew arrived at the shop in February, I felt as though we were all interconnected. We formed an immediate bond, thanks to Tara. We could tell that these people were coming from the right place—from the heart. The energy in the store that day was incredible. There was excitement and static energy in the air between the customers and the crew and Sandy and me. We later went back to our home, where Sandy, Deanna, Helen (Sandy's mom), and I were all to be interviewed and tell our story. They filmed us for hours, asking questions and expressing appreciation for our cooperation.

Eventually, it was Deanna's turn to be filmed. Keep in mind that Deanna did not like talking about feelings and especially about the loss of her sister. This subject always stirred up such anger and sadness in her. The film crew spent about one hour asking Deanna questions about her relationship with Tara and the special things that she and Tara did together. They also had many questions about Deanna's angelic experiences. Sandy and I were hidden off in a corner during this questioning, and we listened intently to Deanna's responses. We were amazed at everything Deanna had to share. We had not heard Deanna open up this much since the loss of Tara. Her responses were meaningful, touching, and deep.

As tears streamed down our faces from the emotion that Deanna's words evoked, we felt so fortunate and overjoyed that she had the opportunity to express herself with this film crew. If for no other reason than allowing Deanna to speak openly about her feelings, this project was worthwhile. Deanna must have felt so comfortable and trusting of these people to open up this way. I thank Tara and the angels for this opportunity, which was a very healing experience for Deanna. This was just another way that we felt Tara was a guiding force from the other realm. It seemed as if she had a way of coordinating events and people and would place them in our lives at the right time for our highest good. We were acting out her message and the message deep within our own hearts.

It often appeared that just when things got comfortable, we would get a kick in the pants to move forward on our journey. Each event seemed to segue into the next in perfect harmony. The week after the filming, the retail store upstairs from our shop became available. This was the prime space in the plaza—on the street, very visible, and larger than our existing space. I suddenly remembered my comment to the landlord before we had opened in September when I was trying to convince him of our idea for the angel store. I had told him that it was my vision to be in that prime space and that someday our shop would be a landmark. I had expressed this at the time with a deep passion.

Now it was only natural that we move into this new space and become more visible to the public as we helped enlighten people about angels. Since we had proven ourselves in the previous five months, the landlord agreed to rent us the new space. We moved into our new shop in March, and it made an incredible difference in our attempt to get Tara's story and the angels out into the world. The one thing I had been concerned about was the energy and presence that people felt in the original store. Would that still be evident? Would people feel that same sense of love and compassion upon entering the new store? My concerns were unnecessary. Everyone who was attracted to the store still felt a wonderful presence when visiting the space. I came to learn that Sandy and I were part of that experience and that the love that was contained within the four walls was not only Tara's but also ours, and it would follow wherever we went.

The Pieces of the Puzzle Start to Come Together

About two weeks later, I received a call from Rex, who told me that the NBC television network saw the angel project they had filmed and wanted it for a two-hour nationwide television special. Rex and his partners were asked to lengthen it, and they needed to shoot more footage in our store and of Sandy, Deanna, and me. Tara was definitely a co-creator in this project. She had always wanted to be an actress or model and be in front of millions of people. She had a message. I marveled at how all the pieces of life were coming together and creating a new picture. I felt an electric energy as this episode of our lives unfolded. I was awed at the roles that we all were playing. The filming was completed by the end of March, and we were told that the special would air on May 24 at 8:00 P.M. Prime time!

We were continuing to learn lessons about people and life. Someone had told us some time before that we would probably see some of our old friendships dropping by the wayside, and at this point in our lives we were indeed losing some of our long-time relationships. I didn't know the exact reasons for this; I could only speculate based on my deep sense of intuition. I knew we were on a path of discovery, adventure, influence, and purpose. Some people couldn't seem to understand or cope with the success and notoriety we were experiencing. After surviving such a great tragedy, we were moving forward. We had chosen to overcome this major adversity in our life and turn it into something that would benefit others through hope and inspiration. We chose to be strong, step out, and put ourselves on the line by making a statement about life, love, and God's plan, which we are all a part of. Doing this might have been threatening to some who were not at the same point in their evolution. This isn't to say that they're wrong, but each of us is at a different stage in our development. We made a choice to allow the angels to protect us, guide us, and support us in our journey. They are messengers of God. Although we were forming new friendships, nothing could replace the old ones and their many cherished memories. Although we can understand from a spiritual vantage why things like this happen, it is still painful. But once again, we grow from these lessons.

The next couple of months passed quickly, each busier than the last. We were amazed at the growth of our business as our store's reputation expanded and the visibility of our new location brought in more customers. As May 24 approached, it suddenly occurred to us that Tara's story would soon be aired nationwide. We did not have the opportunity to see the finished documentary before it aired. Although we trusted the producers and believed in their integrity, we still experienced fear of the unknown. Deeper down, we knew that we had done the right thing, and we were sure Tara would be pleased with the final project.

The show was to air on Tuesday evening at 8:00 P.M. We were asked by NBC if we would like to do some brief "live" interviews, via satellite, on various morning talk shows to help promote the airing of the special. We gladly accepted and were told that we would be picked up in a limousine very early Monday morning and taken to NBC studios in Hollywood to be televised. This was very exciting for us, especially since neither Sandy nor I had ever ridden in a limousine. I believe this was another gift from Tara. Sandy and I had said a number of times that we would enjoy the luxury of riding in a limo.

We arrived at the studio and were immediately ushered into a makeup room and then into a very small soundproof room with two chairs and a television camera. The producers and camera people explained what was going to happen. We would be shooting thirty- to sixty-second segments for about twenty-five different television stations throughout the country. The host of each show would ask us questions after a brief segment of the special was previewed. We could only hear these questions through the tiny earphones we were wearing.

They could see us, but we could not see them. We just looked straight into the camera. We would film one and then have a short break. This continued for about two hours. It was rather tiring to repeat this again and again as we attempted to present ourselves in a calm light. We were successful in carrying out our mission. As we were driven back home, the countdown, as we called it, began: less than thirty-six hours until the special airing.

7

The Touch of an Angel

It is through our greatest tragedies
that we have the opportunities for our greatest growth.
As we overcome adversity and share our knowledge,
other individuals will benefit.

Tuesday, May 24, 1994: Sandy and I were working in the shop all day, anticipating the show that night at 8:00 P.M. At about 4:30 P.M. I suggested that Sandy go on home, and I would close up at 5:30 by myself. Business had been very slow that day, which made the time pass even more slowly. There wasn't a soul in the store between 4:30 and 5:30. At about 5:15, I realized how peaceful and comforting it was in the shop at that moment. There was just me, and all these angels. I felt a presence watching me. Behind the counter where I was standing, a portrait of Tara hung on the wall. I turned around and looked at her smiling face and spoke to her. "Well, Tara, tonight the whole country will know your story. I hope this is what you wanted. I have a feeling that our lives will never be the same."

Not thirty seconds after I said this, the phone rang. It was a man from Florida who was in the hospital. He had just seen our segment on the television special. It had never occurred to me that the show was already airing on the East Coast! The man on the phone was in tears and very touched by our story. He was very kind to me and said how moved he was by our experience. We said good-bye, and I hung up the phone. Immediately it rang again. This time it was a woman from New York calling to express her thoughts about our story. The phone rang again. This time it was a young woman in her twenties, who said she hadn't intended to watch this show, but when she was flipping through the channels her television set got stuck on NBC and she immediately became entranced with Tara. Every time I tried to hang up the phone and leave for home, someone else called. I managed to close the shop after taking some twenty calls. I finally left the phone ringing. My heart was pounding in anticipation of finally getting to see the show, especially after all these calls. I thought the show must be something really amazing. I realized that Sandy and I must have gotten so used to our experience that it was not so astounding to us at this point. However, other people seemed to be deeply affected by it.

I got in the car and started my drive home. The car phone rang, and it was Sandy. She was worried because

I was late, and she said that something must be wrong with the phone at the shop; she had been trying to call me there but only got a busy signal. I explained about all the incoming calls, and she was amazed. She, too, had received a couple of calls from acquaintances on the East Coast who had already viewed the special. It was then that I began to realize the magnitude of what we had created. It never occurred to me the monumental proportions this whole event would take.

As eight o'clock approached, Sandy, Deanna, and I positioned ourselves in front of the television. We had found out only a short time earlier that our segment was the opening story. I remember thinking that it was just like Tara to be the opening act. She really wanted to make a statement. We sat with our eyes glued to the set as Patty Duke, the hostess of the show, introduced our segment. We watched as our story unfolded in a new light. There was Tara's beautiful face filling the screen and Deanna speaking intelligently and honestly. Pictures of our family growing up together flashed in a montage on the screen—the vacations, the birthday parties, the love we shared as a family. My eyes welled up with tears, which eventually streamed down my face. As I looked over at Sandy and Deanna, I saw the same emotion pouring from them. Tara's story, our story, could not have been told any better or with more compassion. The essence of our love and understanding for one another had been captured perfectly. We were all so moved by the production that we sat in silence for a moment, not knowing what to say. We went to sleep that night feeling relieved at the outcome and wondering if the community and public had felt the specialness of our experience.

I arrived the next day at the store only to begin to realize how much our lives were about to change. My journey would be accelerated from this point, sometimes going so fast and furiously that I would feel consumed. However, my purpose on this planet would become more obvious with each passing day.

It was about 8:30 A.M. when I walked into the store. The red light of the answering machine was blinking erratically. It had reached its capacity for saving messages. As I started to retrieve the messages, the phone began to ring—again one call after the other. Each person who called had something to share along with expressing how moved they were with our story. I was unable to retrieve any of the messages or even prepare for the store to open at 10:00 A.M. Everyone who called was kind and wonderful and moved to tears as we spoke. Some people began telling me of their own personal angel experiences that had occurred years ago, which they had never felt safe sharing until now, with a total stranger.

One woman, a single parent of a nine-year-old daughter, called from Chicago and shared the heartwarming experience that she and her daughter had experienced after watching our story. She said her daughter had always worried about her mother's safety and feared that she might someday be left alone. However, after seeing the story of Tara and her family, she somehow felt safe and comforted about her mother and herself being alone. The mother was overjoyed by the more secure feeling her daughter had and was very thankful that we had had the courage to share our lives and affect hers in such a manner. She asked if there was a book or anything that she could buy and have mailed to her daughter. I assured her that I had a wonderful children's book that included an angel necklace perfect for a nine-year-old girl. I was so touched by the woman's compassion and sincerity that I felt moved to send her the book and a Tara's Angels T-shirt with no thought of being reimbursed. Interestingly enough, we had only one T-shirt remaining in the store, and it was tucked back in a closet. It was a small (normally we only carry these in adult sizes). There are no accidents, and I know this was truly a gift from Tara. I would discover as time went on how deeply not just adults but children were touched by the story of Tara and her angels.

The stories and experiences I continued to hear that morning were unbelievable. When the doors of the shop opened that morning at 10:30, people began pouring in while the telephone rang nonstop. Sandy and I took turns waiting on customers and answering the phone. It was a beautiful sight, but also overwhelming. Neither of us had realized the impact the show would have on our business. I hadn't realized that the death of Tara and the events that surrounded our experience with her and the angels would send such a universal message. Everyone entering the store wanted to talk and share their support. They were in tears, and so were we. The information operator eventually got through to us and said that their switchboards were overloaded with inquiries about our phone number. They wanted to know what was going on. The Chamber of Commerce called and told us that they, too, had been inundated with calls. Then the producers at NBC television called to tell us the same story. By the end of the day, we were exhausted. Sandy and I looked at each other and wondered what this was all about. We knew we were the vehicles to get a message out to the world, yet we were unprepared for this kind of response. With the exception of a couple of part-time employees, Sandy and I were the only ones operating the store. We went home that evening anticipating what the rest of the week might bring.

The next day, Thursday, was busier than the previous day. The phone rang constantly, and people kept filling the store. Friday was busier still. Then came the weekend. People were lined up outside the store on Saturday. We asked one of our employees to do nothing but answer the phone all day—primarily to give directions to the store. The lines stretched from the counter to outside the entrance. Of course, everyone wanted to talk and express their love just before leaving with their purchase. Sandy and I did not know where we were getting the energy to keep going. Everyone we met was kind and compassionate. I was truly amazed at the number of people who had had angel experiences but had chosen not to share them until they felt safe.

Although we were having difficulty keeping our minds clear with all the chaos, we began to realize that we were living our purpose at this very moment. This phenomenon was not about a retail store but about providing a safe place for people to have feelings. There are so many people in pain and uncertainty. Many people feel they are alone with their ideas and beliefs. People have become disillusioned with life and want to feel there is something more. They want to feel inspired to overcome the adversities in their lives. People want to feel loved and accepted.

Little did we know that we were providing an opportunity for so many people to reach out to someone or something tangible that could give them hope.

That first week, we received over two thousand phone calls (those were the ones that got through) from around the country. We had people driving from other states just to visit our store and meet us. Two couples drove from Canada. Many of the people who called or came into the shop had lost a loved one. Quite a few had lost a child. I was surprised at how many of them said they felt comforted by our experience, knowing that there was another existence after death and that their departed loved one was on the other side. This struck me as odd, because Sandy and I have always known that life is eternal and that the soul or spirit lives forever. We assumed that the majority of people thought the same way, but we found that we had confirmed this for many. It was apparent that we had reached numerous people on many different levels. Although Sandy and I were absolutely frazzled by the close of business Sunday evening, I could sense Tara smiling upon us and saying that she was so proud of what we were doing. I could sense her thanking us for being her parents.

How come Monday morning is so close to Sunday evening? I drove to the shop in a daze, wondering what the day would bring. When I entered the store, I realized that we had depleted most of our merchandise. We were so unprepared for the onslaught that had besieged us the previous week that our inventory was wiped out. I made an effort to rearrange things so the store wouldn't look so empty.

Once again the phones were ringing. The answering machine finally broke due to the overload of calls, and people were peering in the windows. All the attention was miraculous and appreciated but still exhausting. At this point Sandy and I had asked our part-time employees to become full-time as we knew we were unable to do it all. Friends had volunteered to answer phones and help greet people. A customer, who was a godsend, even started answering the phone for us, giving people directions.

While Sandy was on the phone ordering merchandise, I realized that we needed something additional—more space. The shop next door to us had been vacant for about three months. Sandy and I looked at it and realized simultaneously that we needed this space. We weren't sure what we could do with it, but we knew that we needed to create another shop for the many people that now knew our story. We needed to expand. We went to the landlord and signed the lease for the new space.

Then we received another sign of how the universe works for us and guides us in new directions. Sometimes we don't know where we are headed, but if we listen to our instincts or intuition and don't worry about the outcome, we find our path is correct. The day after we signed the lease, I received a phone call from the artist Andy Lakey. He had also appeared on the angel special that we were on. He told us that he was touched very deeply by our story and said he wanted to meet with us that next Friday to discuss an idea with us. Of course, we accepted.

The week sped by with the crowds still streaming through the store. We could not keep the store stocked with merchandise. Our method of running our business was taking on a new dimension. Sandy and I did not want to take any days off because so many people were traveling great distances to come and meet us. We felt a responsibility to be there to talk with them. When Friday rolled around, we did take the afternoon off to meet with Andy Lakey.

Andy had had a very profound experience several years previously when he had overdosed on drugs and almost died. He found himself in the presence of angels, who surrounded him with unconditional love. As this was occurring, he asked for his life back and in turn promised he would seek help and rehabilitate himself.

He also promised to do something to help humanity. The angels told him to paint, something he had never done in his life. He was told that he must paint two thousand angel paintings by the year 2000 and that he would be guided in his technique. He followed their instructions and attracted quite a bit of attention over the next few years. Numerous people collect his work, and his paintings have an essence that captures people's hearts.

When we arrived at Andy's home, we marveled at the paintings that adorned the walls. Each painting had a dramatic effect on both Sandy and me. Andy sat down and looked at us, and the first words out of his mouth were, "You have been chosen." Chosen for what? I thought. Of course, these words had a very familiar ring, as I had heard them before from the angelic beings I had encountered earlier. Chills ran through my body. I felt as if Andy were looking deep into my soul when he spoke. I felt validated, and I knew that this was spirit talking to spirit.

Andy went on to say that he had been looking for someone to run a gallery in Southern California for his artwork. He wanted it to be someone with integrity. Since he donated five percent of the proceeds from the sale of his paintings to children's organizations, he wanted someone to match this five percent donation for a total of ten percent. Now my mind was whirling. For my whole life, I had had a dream of being able to give support to children's foundations. Here was an opportunity for my vision to be fulfilled. More pieces of the puzzle were falling into place, and the experiences in my life were starting to make more and more sense. When Andy asked us to be a gallery for his work, we told him how we had just leased an additional store with no idea of exactly what we were going to do with it. And, amazingly enough, this new space had the ideal floor plan for an art gallery!

We began preparations immediately for the new store. Crowds of people continued to fill the existing store as we decorated the new store. We wanted a heavenly feel in the new store, but even more we wanted to convey an ethereal essence and Renaissance feeling. It was once again amazing how when we asked for something, it made itself known. One morning I mentioned to Sandy how I had envisioned a mural on the ceiling with angels of the Renaissance era looking down. This image appeared so clearly in my mind that I could already see it in place. About an hour after I got to the shop, a woman stopped by the store and introduced herself. She said, "I don't know exactly why I stopped by your store, but I just had an urge to talk to you about something I do."

Well, by this time I was getting used to people sharing their unusual experiences, so this did not surprise me. I listened as she continued and then my jaw dropped as she spoke her next few words: "I paint murals with angels that have a feeling of the Renaissance era, and I thought that perhaps I could be of service to you." I couldn't believe what I was hearing; no less than two hours before I had affirmed what she was now suggesting. The universe was once again responding synchronistically to my requests and showing me that all I had to do was ask. The artist had her portfolio with her, and as I glanced at her work, I could see that it was exactly what I had wanted.

I realized that there was more at work here than I could see physically. I came to the conclusion that Tara was planting ideas not just in my mind but in the minds of others as well, and now these ideas were taking form. This phenomenon was growing bigger than I had ever imagined, but still it had to be part of the mission. Everything was happening so quickly, and our lives were accelerating faster than we could keep up. God and the angels were moving at a pace that I found difficult to maintain. I kept thinking, "We are only human and can only do so much in a given period of time." I guess their message was so important that they needed to move the process along. Tara was in the consciousness of so many people, and on any given day we heard endless accounts from people all over the country who told us that Tara had come to them with a message or an inspiration.

Sandy and I were exhausted from all the attention and exposure we were receiving. With the preparation of the new store and the constant activity of the existing store, we decided we needed to start hiring more employees. We had three part-time people working in the store and offered them full-time employment, which they accepted. We then hired an administrative assistant to handle the phone calls and bookkeeping and a myriad of other duties. Then we began filling positions in the second store and ordering new merchandise.

It was very evident that we were overworked and needed a break. Ever since we had taken Tara and Jen to Kauai, I had been yearning to take Deanna there and show her all the wonderful places that we had discovered two years before. Fortunately, Sandy and I had scheduled some vacation time in Hanalei Bay, Kauai, that summer. The new store was to open July 30, and our vacation was planned for the last week in June and the first week in July. The timing of this vacation was perfect to allow us to renew ourselves before the grand opening. I was very excited about sharing this wonderful place with Deanna for the first time. I could hardly wait to return to my paradise—this paradise from what seemed like another lifetime.

8

My Life Becomes
an Open Book

We all approach life in a special way.
Allow your feelings and opinions to be known.
They are important.

As more and more people approached us to tell us that
Tara had come to them with a message or that Tara had
inspired them, I found that I felt emotionally void. This
was my daughter they were speaking of, my daughter
who was instantly killed in an automobile accident
nearly two years before. How was I supposed to feel?
Touched by the fact that Tara was influencing so many
others, or sad because she was not here in the physical
form and I was missing out on the rest of my life with
her as I had planned it? I had unknowingly placed a protective shield around me so I would not be vulnerable or
acknowledge fully the reality of what had happened.
Maybe I completely understood the spiritual blueprint
but was confused by the human emotions that existed

side by side. Sometimes it is very difficult being a spiritual being in a human body on this plane of existence.

Just a few weeks prior to the new store opening, a very kind woman approached us and said she needed to meet with Sandy and me along with some other people she would invite to convey a message that was very important. This woman, Beverly, was very calm and credible, and she had an air of universal wisdom and confidence. The invitation was calm yet urgent, as if it were for our highest good. We agreed to meet in the existing store one evening after hours since Tara's energy was so strong. In fact people had stated that there was an energy vortex present in the store. Beverly brought with her two individuals who had a gift of receiving messages from the other side through their own receptivity. Sandy and I are very openminded people who neither condemn nor condone others for their beliefs or philosophies. We try not to be judgmental, as we know all people are on their own paths at their own paces, and we are all searching for the same thing.

As we gathered that evening with Beverly and her two friends, Sandy, Deanna, and I anxiously awaited their message. Tara's energy was very strong that evening, and it was obvious that her spirit was present. As the communication began, there was no question that it was Tara. What they said convinced Sandy and me it could only be Tara. Here were two total strangers conveying messages and making statements that could only have meaning to Sandy and me. Tara was saying how proud she was of all that Sandy and I were doing and that she was always with us and in the store and wherever she needed to be. In the angelic realm, the spirit is so magnified that it is possible to be in many places at once. With our limited knowledge, it's difficult to conceive of this possibility. Sandy and I know that this was Tara's presence because the room was filled with the purest essence of love. Tara stated that where she is, love is what is most important. Her next message communicated a profound truth: God is all there is, and we are it! We were all moved to tears, including Deanna. I kept analyzing what was going on, somehow questioning or trying to discredit it. But the feeling and presence in the room were undeniable.

Then came a familiar message: "You have been chosen for a mission." As these words were spoken, Sandy and I looked at each other. My mind immediately flashed to my experience when I was nine, which I didn't recall until some thirty-three years later when I heard these words during my hypnotherapy session. Then I had heard them again from Andy Lakey just a few weeks ago. Now they were being spoken yet again. What more validation could I ask for? Of course, I asked, "What is the mission?" although I had a fairly good idea at this point. We had been chosen at some time in our evolution to be a role model or influence for people in overcoming adversity, living with unconditional love and integrity, and not being judgmental; this was part of the path we had agreed upon. I knew this, but I wanted to hear it from another source. With the help of God, Tara, and the angels, we had created a safe and loving environment for people from every walk of life to come and express their feelings. We were helping open people's consciousness to the fact that there is a greater power and that we all have the potential of achieving what we put our minds to and our hearts in.

My heart continued to palpitate as the messages flowed forward. I was told to write of my experiences, which up until then I had pretty much kept to myself. I wondered about this, since I had never written anything, although I knew I had had enough experiences to make a book. I am basically a humble person, and to write a book about my experience seemed to be a monumental task. I said that I would need some assistance with this endeavor. What should I do? The room got very still and quiet as we all remained motionless for a moment. Then, for no apparent reason, a book leaped off the shelf onto the floor. We all looked at one another as we were startled out of our chairs. I went over to pick up the book. I grew pale and speechless as all eyes were on me. I told everyone that the title of the book was *Messengers of Light* by Terry Lynn Taylor.

The bookcase that this book had fallen from was a few feet from the table where we were all sitting and had not been disturbed by anyone. The five-shelf bookcase was filled with at least thirty different titles that the store carries. Yet this one book miraculously made itself known, for a reason. Tara was trying to convey to me that I should talk to Terry Lynn Taylor about the book that I was to write. The author who had so entranced Tara and allowed her to connect with the angelic realm was to help me write my own book. The idea seemed very natural to me, especially since I had spoken to Terry on the phone and in person half a dozen times during the past few months. Since I had never written anything other than short stories in college, I thought that perhaps Terry was going to co-author a book with me. Later I would find out that her help would take another form.

I realized I knew that this book was something that had to be written. I remembered that after the airing of the television special, people had come to the shop and asked for the book about Tara and our experience with the angels. How odd that so many people had asked for a book that hadn't been written yet! Where did they get the idea that there was a book? Every situation kept leading to another situation, and I began to see the entire picture of this puzzle. The pieces were coming together much faster now. The evening ended with all of us inspired by what had happened. The clarity, love, and understanding were helping us make sense of what our experience was all about. But why was I having such tormenting feelings, feelings that were causing me to question if I wanted to continue on this path I had chosen?

I realized that the joy I had created with the one aspect of my life was being overshadowed by the feelings I was experiencing in my solitude. Again, human emotions often coexist beside spiritual awareness; this is the great paradox of human existence. The more I tried to be content with the business we had created, the more I realized that I had been trying to conceal my turmoil. At times I felt as if I was not living and that nothing I did really mattered. I missed Tara so deeply, and I missed my family as I had known it. I felt that I no longer had a family structure and that I was just existing from day to day with no real purpose. I was dead inside. I felt this deadness in everything I did, although I was good at masking this side of myself to everyone, except Sandy. I began losing my ambition. I didn't care about things that were previously important to me, and I was void of any feelings.

I wanted to run away and hide. The direction I had intended for my life would never be. I missed the family vacations. I missed the way the four of us enjoyed life and one another. It felt as if Sandy, Deanna, and I were all going in different directions. With one integral part of our family missing, the basic dynamics of our interaction had changed. Sandy felt alone, Deanna felt deserted, and I couldn't fix it. I sensed that Deanna had some built-up anger toward me. I felt as though she thought I didn't like her and that in some way she thought that I would have preferred to lose her rather than Tara. I wanted so many times to talk to her about this, but I could not find the strength to bring the subject up. How could a child think such a thought? It hurt me a great deal to think that Deanna was feeling this way. All I could do was wait for time to heal this wound and hope that Deanna would realize the truth of my feelings.

The store had kept us so busy that I hadn't had time to pay attention to my feelings until we hired more employees and my schedule lightened enough for me to face reality. All the wonderful things that had happened no longer seemed to be enough. Sandy and I had always enjoyed an outstanding relationship. Although we had grown closer in some ways since Tara's death, we had also created some distance between us. This was nothing that couldn't be resolved, but we were both so exhausted that it was an effort to try any harder to make things better. Every time we went out to dinner, we would reflect on our life and break down in tears in the midst of our meal. Despite our grief, we persisted in following our path and striving to fulfill our purpose.

In realizing that I needed to proceed with writing a book, I decided to contact Terry Lynn Taylor to set up a meeting. I had written the first couple of pages to show Terry and explain the general theme. I told her that I knew she was somehow going to be involved with this book and that I needed her input and assistance. I asked her if she would co-author the book since I was not a known writer. We met one morning, and I read her the first two pages I had written. She adamantly told me that I must write the book myself. She said I was a very good writer, and that it must be my story. I was a little confused because I had gotten a sign that she was somehow connected with this book. Now I didn't know how she was to be involved. I'm sure my disappointment showed. But then she went on to say, "Why don't I talk to my publisher about this book and see if they have any interest in publishing it." Her words were very encouraging, as I could now see the link between Terry, the book, and her publisher. H J Kramer, the publisher of *Messengers of Light,* was indeed to be the publisher of my book. Terry's words of support—"You must write this story"—remained with me as we traveled to Kauai. I was extremely inspired, and I began writing my book.

When we arrived in Kauai, Sandy and I felt as if we had never left. We felt as if time had been frozen, and we were where we belonged. Deanna and her friend Danielle were as much in love with this island as Sandy and I were. Nothing essential had changed, even though there had been a devastating hurricane two years before. We hiked in the hills and swam in the ocean and loved being in the presence of nature's beauty. Everything brought back loving memories of Tara. Every path we walked and every activity we shared with Deanna touched my heart as I felt the absence of Tara. I have never regretted anything in my life except that Deanna had not been part of our vacation with Tara two years prior. There must have been some reason.

I was becoming obsessed with Kauai. Sandy loved the island, too, but I had a particularly strong need to be there. Since Tara's Angels was now nationally known, we had received many requests for a franchise. How do you franchise an "experience"? Our store was not just a retail shop. The idea of opening another store only seemed inviting if we were to do it in Kauai. Since we had had a wonderful experience with Tara in Kauai, one of our last, and since this island is very spiritual, it seemed a natural progression. We contacted a real estate agent and decided to see what retail space was available. There was a new building that had just one space available—here we go again—which was the same size and configuration as our original store. The only difference was that this store looked out on magnificent green mountains with a cascading waterfall and endless taro fields. The rent was similar, and everything seemed right. We took a copy of the lease with us and told the agent that we would have to discuss it with our accountant to ensure that this would all make sense financially.

The two weeks we spent in Kauai with Deanna were rejuvenating. We took Deanna to all the special places that we had visited with Tara. As we stood on one of the most beautiful beaches that we had discovered while there with Tara, Deanna, Sandy, and I felt the gentle breeze renewing us and comforting us as we eyed the awesome view. I could feel Tara's presence of love and beauty as we allowed our senses to be overcome with this moment. There was no doubt in my mind that we were in the right place at the right moment. We had a strong desire to just be here at this place in this moment. This island would become a haven to us for years to come, and a calling from some higher power.

One evening while looking out at the bay with the moon reflecting on the water, Deanna and I talked and shared about some fun family times we had experienced together. It got to be late, and Deanna looked at the digital clock and said, "Look, it's 11:11. Let's make a wish." I agreed, of course, and then asked, "What does that mean, 11:11?" And then Deanna shared with me that many times when she and Tara could not fall asleep they would climb into each other's bed and talk. Deanna said that Tara had told her that when the clock read 11:11, they had to make a wish, and that 11:11 was very special. Tara never explained why, but it made Deanna feel good to make a wish with Tara. She said that Tara had repeated this whenever they were together at 11:11. Deanna went on to explain that this was a fun way to end the evening with Tara; they were alone in the darkness of the night, and the huge numbers on the clock would flash 11:11. I asked Deanna how long she and Tara had been doing this, and she said for a few months prior to the accident.

I could tell Deanna missed this special game that Tara had taught her. I thought what a wonderful memory for Deanna to hold onto—something so special that bonded the two of them together. Interestingly enough, I would discover a few months later that 11:11 had an even deeper meaning than I had realized.

Upon returning to California, we quickly got caught up in the hysteria of the business again. With the lease in hand and a conservative business projection, we approached our accountant and asked him to make an evaluation of our business position to see if it was feasible for us to open a store in Kauai. As the days passed, I began losing interest in opening another store, primarily because I felt all used up and did not have the energy to commit to the work involved. I also felt that from a financial standpoint it was unrealistic. So, I awaited the final word from the accountant, who originally thought that it was probably not the best idea to go through with this venture. About five days later, he met with Sandy and me and said, to my amazement, "I don't see any reason not to go forward with a store in Kauai."

My jaw dropped as he made this statement. I guess I was hoping that someone else would make a decision for me, but now all signs were pointing in the same direction: to go forward with this plan. We became so consumed with opening the second store and all that went with it that we made no immediate decision. I didn't want to say no, and I didn't want to say yes. We had even met someone in Kauai who was prepared to manage the store for us. All the indicators were in place, but I still couldn't say yes. Opening the second store was such a drain on us physically and financially that we discarded any thought of opening another store, no matter how right it might feel. We couldn't jeopardize our health and financial stability. We knew that having a store in Kauai was right but the timing was wrong. Things would happen when they were supposed to. "Learn to just be and not always do. Take deep breaths and meditate." I kept hearing this good advice from people. I wanted so much to live by these standards, but I often felt anxious about moving forward—anxious for the next step. With the way my life had changed so dramatically, I was no longer content with "everyday" life. There had to be a purpose and a vision, and there was. I felt I was living from one adventure to the next. Everything was happening too fast. The store in Kauai would have to wait.

With the opening of our second store in San Capistrano, the business had gotten to be so demanding that many times Sandy and I felt that things were out of control. As I mentioned before, this wasn't just a retail venture; it was a place where we needed to be present to talk to people and listen and support them. We realized that by opening ourselves up to the public, we had created this for ourselves. It was okay, but we were unprepared for the magnitude of what we had spawned.

As the pace of running two stores increased, we discovered again that some of our long-term friendships were falling by the wayside. Certain people couldn't understand what we were doing or why we were doing it. Bottom line, I think that they thought we had "lost it." Our path was headed in a different direction now, and we were growing. Others were satisfied with their lives as they were. We have always supported and honored our friends in their journey and their lives, but we were not receiving the same support from all of them. People tend to look at you differently when you have lost a child. It makes them question their own immortality. We had chosen to view this experience as a lesson and an opportunity for growth. This can be threatening to some, although we also had many friends who supported and nurtured us on our journey. While it hurt deeply to lose old friendships, we were also discovering many new friendships that would prove to be on a much deeper level.

All people have gifts within them that they bring into this lifetime. Sandy and I have always tried to be aware of the good within people and emphasize or support that attribute. Between our two stores and our office, there were now nine employees working for us, each of whom possessed a special talent for what we needed. It appeared as if we had all the right people in the right places. One of our most valuable employees was our office administrator. She was a friend we had known through church. She had been laid off from a job just two days after we had leased the second store. There couldn't have been a more perfect person for the administrative position, and the timing was just right. I sensed that Tara, once again, participated in the synchronicity of these events.

Tara seemed to know what was needed more than we did, and although I usually tried to listen to the intuition that I was receiving from her, sometimes I did not. We ended up giving too much authority to one individual we hired, and that almost cost us the business. I had felt from the initial interview that this person was not right. There was something that made me feel uncomfortable. I questioned my feelings, however, and having nothing to validate my uncertainty, I decided not to follow my intuition. After about three months, we discovered some problems. Fortunately, we parted ways, but the aftereffects of this situation were serious. We made it through this rough period, but not without an enormous amount of stress.

This was a difficult lesson, but I was learning to listen to my intuition and not let my ego get in the way. I discovered a saying that would help me to understand and listen to my feelings and intuitions: "Angels are God's thoughts passing to humanity." Don't question the outcome; just follow your heart. This lesson was also about not giving up our power and thinking that someone else, who did not hold the big picture, had more knowledge than we did in running a business. Sandy and I talked about never allowing anyone to extract our powers and remembering that we knew, consciously or subconsciously, what was best for our business. This is our business, and we are the guiding force behind it.

During this time, we began to get phone calls from some talk shows. It was always amazing to me how things kept mushrooming. At home one afternoon, we received a call from the *Oprah Winfrey Show*, which wanted us to be a guest on a show they were doing about angel experiences. I had always had the highest regard for Ms. Winfrey. I felt her integrity so clearly that I was disappointed when the show decided not to use us. However, there is a reason for everything, and evidently the timing was not right for us or her at that moment. We did receive a call from the *Leeza* show to appear and discuss our experience, and Deanna was included as well. Once again we were the opening guests, and the show went very well. It aired just two days prior to the rebroadcast of the NBC television special "Angels: The Mysterious Messengers." Because the original airing had had such high ratings, NBC decided to air the show a second time. These two shows sent a flurry of people to the shop again. A Brazilian television network, which has a show equivalent to the American television show *20/20,* interviewed us one afternoon. Tara's message was continuing to make itself known, now internationally, and our path was unfolding clearly once again.

As more and more attention was being brought to our stores, we found that Andy Lakey's artwork and Tara's Angels formed a perfect union. Mr. Lakey's paintings were selling steadily, and we were delighted to be making donations to children's foundations. There was something so purposeful in contributing to organizations that empowered children in the surrounding community. This aspect of our life was a dream come true. A television show called *Sightings* came to the shop and filmed

Andy Lakey and us discussing the effect his artwork has on people and how we were all divinely guided with our endeavors. With the recognition we were receiving, our gallery was turning into one of Andy Lakey's fastest growing galleries in the country. With his energy and our energy working in conjunction, the studio was creating so much good for so many people.

One of the visions that Sandy and I had always had since the inception of the store was to create a weekly meeting called "The Gathering of Angels," a forum for people from all walks of life to get together to discuss angels and learn from one another about angels and what they represent. However, neither Sandy nor I had the time or the energy to conduct these sessions. Suddenly an idea flashed. There was a wonderful lady, Debbie Wilmon, who had arranged for us to go to an angel conference earlier in the year. She, too, had had an angel experience. Everything in life is so synchronistic with people whose paths cross. We had experienced an immediate bond with Debbie when we first met, and now here was an opportunity to call on her wisdom and talents to be part of our shop. We talked to Debbie about being the facilitator, and she accepted immediately.

The gatherings started meeting on Wednesday evenings in the gallery section of the second store. The idea was not to have any rigid format but to allow people to share and feel comfortable in expressing whatever moved them. Each meeting proved to be magical in some way. There were those who attended regularly, but there were always new participants arriving each week. Sandy and I attended along with Debbie, who demonstrated her innate talent for conducting these gatherings. Each week people would leave the gatherings with a special feeling of enlightenment and a new understanding of the angels' love, hope, and inspiration. Every meeting evolved into another unique expression of our shop.

Somehow, and I don't know how, the nightly television show *Extra* got wind of our "Gathering of Angels" and wanted to film a segment for their show. Sandy and I have watched this show on a regular basis and found it odd that they would want us to appear in a segment. The show typically has a format of current information about celebrities and the entertainment industry. I was flattered that they had contacted us, but I kept asking the producers why they wanted to film us; we weren't celebrities. Their response was that someone affiliated with the show wanted a segment on angels, and we were chosen. They continued to say that, in some ways, we were celebrities. Well, I went along with this, and we proceeded to set up a time for the filming. I just figured that Tara had planted this idea somewhere to get more exposure on another level. The power of angels!

9

Trusting in the Divine Plan

Always do the best you can
and then let go, leaving the rest to God and the angels.
For it is with their love and wisdom
that they will act on your behalf.

A few days prior to the filming of our "Gathering of Angels," I received a very interesting phone call from a man who lives in Studio City, California. He said he was a stuntman for the movies. He also told me that he was a clairvoyant and often received messages from different sources. Since we had received many such calls, I wasn't surprised at his initial statement. He said he had gotten a message from someone called Tara and was told to call our store. He asked me if Tara had ever been interested in angels and had ever made a cookie. Then he proceeded to ask me if there was any relationship with surfing (Deanna's favorite sport and one of her connections with Tara). I was not too impressed at this point, because I thought that he had seen the television special. This information was common knowledge. Then he asked me who Tara was. I told him that Tara was my daughter and that she had been killed in an automobile accident and that she had developed a deep love for angels. He responded as if he knew nothing of our store or our experience of Tara's fate. I found this conversation puzzling and wondered what his point was. Then he made a very interesting statement that left me dumbfounded. He said, "There is something about a film or the film industry, and Tara is watching over the film industry regarding a movie." I didn't know what to say. I had always thought that perhaps an in-depth story of our experience and journey would make an impact on many people, but I had not discussed this subject with anyone to date. I did not know what to make of this conversation. The man was very kind and credible, but to call me out of the blue about making a film defied anything I could have imagined. I thanked him for calling and took his phone number down (which I have since lost), and we said good-bye. I had to process this for a moment, and as I sat in silence I wondered what was truly going on. He spoke with such conviction. I always felt that Tara was coordinating events in some way, but to have a stranger validate this was haunting. His words were implanted in my mind, and I couldn't release them. I wondered what Tara had in mind with this project.

The next weekend, a lovely woman who was a regular customer of our shop came down and brought her grown son who lived in Los Angeles. She introduced Alex to me and left us there to talk while she went shopping. Alex shared with me that his mother had been trying to get him down here for months. She had relayed the story of our store to him and kept telling him that she thought there was a potential movie project based on our story. Alex is a producer in Hollywood. He finally gave into his mother's pleas and came down to see what our store was all about. He had not seen the NBC television special, so he was unfamiliar with our experience. Alex explained his position in the movie industry and said that he had set a goal of bringing integrity back into the movies. He had previously worked on several projects that were not handled this way. He kept a list of affirmations in his wallet of what he hoped to accomplish. I felt an immediate respect for Alex and his ambitions. He asked if we had ever considered our story being told on a larger scale.

I was interested in hearing more, but I was extremely busy that day. I suggested that he somehow obtain a copy of the television special so he could understand the full impact of the story. Our store normally carries the video for sale, but we were out of stock at the time, or so I thought. I went to the back room to get Alex a business card, and there, under a stack of papers, I spied one brand new video that had never been touched. I don't question events like this any longer. Everything is in its right place at the right time. I handed the video to Alex and explained that I didn't know where it had come from, but I knew it was for him. He gladly accepted it and said he would watch it with his partner and contact me at some later time. We said good-bye, and I felt the beginning of a long-term relationship. It's interesting how things always work in accordance with the natural flow of life. And the appearance of Alex and the phone call from the mysterious man a few days prior were part of this natural energy flow.

The film crew from *Extra* was coming that Monday to the store to shoot a segment on the "Gathering of Angels." We contacted some of the individuals who attended regularly to participate in the filming. As the crew wrapped up their shoot, they told us that it would air in one week and would be a four- or five-minute segment.

The next day, I received a call from Alex, who had watched the video. He wanted Sandy and me to come up to Hollywood to meet with him and his partner to discuss the possibility of a project. I was very surprised at how quickly they wanted to pursue this. We met with them two days later in their office. They wanted to throw some ideas around and discuss some options with us. We all discussed the idea of a feature film or a TV movie. Alex and his partner had primarily worked in film, but they felt that perhaps our story might be better suited for a TV movie. We were open to any options, knowing that the right thing would happen. We have learned never to have any expectations on the outcome of a situation; we just let the universe handle it in its own time.

When *Extra* aired one week later, we were again the opening segment, and Tara's smiling face filled the TV screen. They did a beautiful job of including excerpts from the "Gathering of Angels" and showing various statements from the interview that Sandy and I had given them. The co-host of the show closed the segment with a statement that seemed to come out of nowhere. Her words were, "You won't have to wait for Tara and her angels to come down to Earth. Her story will be coming up soon as a TV movie." No one had ever mentioned this possibility to her or to the crew. I have no idea what moved her to say this. I've been told that when you hear something three times, it's going to come true. I felt that not only were we vehicles, but others were being guided, too. I was still amazed when things like this happened, but I was also getting used to it.

As all these events took place, I felt as if I were watching my life happen, but it wasn't really happening to me. It's a very strange thing when people and events come at you and you act or react without thought. Somehow I needed to get grounded and live in the moment, in the now. I see why people with a celebrity status sometimes become reclusive. Sandy and I are not in that same arena, yet we do have a reputation and are very accessible to people. I needed some downtime, and so did Sandy. What Sandy and I had created through Tara's experience was wonderful and purposeful, but we couldn't allow ourselves to be consumed by it. We had to establish our priorities.

The holidays were approaching, and business had barely died off from the summer tourists when people began preparations for Thanksgiving and Christmas. It's interesting how all your life you look forward to these wonderful holidays, then one day something happens to change your whole perspective on this glorious time of year. It appeared that these holidays would never be the same for us. It became a ritual of just getting through them the best we could. We had no extended family to support us or nurture us or try to make the holidays easier for us. It was just the three of us, and we held tightly to one another.

This was the first Christmas we had spent at home since Tara's death. We felt that we had healed enough to face the holidays in a more traditional way; besides, we were too tired to travel this year. We coasted through Christmas Day and even managed to maintain a tradition that we had started in December 1992. On Christmas Day, wherever we were, Sandy, Deanna, and I would each write a letter to Tara. In this letter, we would list something that we would give to Tara as a gift. It could be tangible or intangible. Then we would list something that she would give us. We would then share the letters with one another. This ritual was most difficult for Deanna, who would usually resist it but eventually give in. This tradition always created an emotional outbreak of tears, but we wanted to include Tara and keep her spirit close to us.

New Year's Eve 1994 approached. I always tend to become deeply reflective as we exit one year and enter the next. I pondered all the miraculous events of 1994 and how our lives had changed due to these circumstances. I reviewed the depression and sadness I had felt and still was feeling, trying to determine if there was anything that would make me truly happy. Although I was extremely thankful for all the positive events that had occurred, I still was not satisfied with myself or my life. I looked at the pain that Deanna still carried, and noted that she, too, tried to mask it by not acknowledging Tara. She constantly surrounded herself with friends so as not to feel her loneliness. She was healing, but it was still very difficult for her. Sandy felt lost at times and purposeless. She felt a great deal of responsibility with the store, and she was also missing the family dynamics that were so important to her existence. On the upside, we felt that we were living our purpose and that events in 1995 were going to expand even further. We had a strong sense that we would be doing some lectures and workshops as well as traveling. We had given a few brief talks for a couple of community events in the fall and felt that this area was going to mushroom in 1995. Through all the exposure we had received, we now had a mailing list of fifteen thousand people. These were all people who had either visited the store or phoned us and requested to be on our mailing list. We had such a demand for a catalogue that one of our goals was to print one for mailing in the spring.

With regard to personal goals, we wanted to find peace in our lives. We were hopeful that we could create a new existence that would lend itself to a less chaotic lifestyle. Sandy and I had considered having another child, which was a little risky at our age. We were both in our early forties and very healthy, but having a child would be a much bigger step at this stage in our lives. We discussed this topic thoroughly, making sure that we were wanting a baby for all the right reasons. We were not trying to replace Tara. We never intended to have only one child, and it didn't feel right having just one now. We loved being parents, and we wanted Deanna to have a sibling since we had no real extended family. With our busy lifestyle, we knew that we would have to rearrange our priorities and make some drastic changes. We weighed the options both ways, unable to decide what was right or best for us. Would another child bring renewed joy and a passion for living? Or would having a child be too difficult with the lifestyle that we now had? Could we manage this additional responsibility? We took the easy way out and left it up to the universe to decide. We put no expectations on the outcome and gave it our best shot, knowing what is right will be done.

10

The Never-Ending Mission

If we listen,
we can hear what our heart is saying.
If we open our eyes,
we will take the right steps to follow that voice.
Find your purpose!

The new year had no sooner come and gone than we started getting requests for speaking engagements and workshops. People seemed to want to hear our story firsthand over and over again. We developed an interactive workshop that gave people the opportunity to learn about themselves and others through sharing, working in groups, and completing work sheets we had prepared. Sandy and I were again guided and given the opportunity to provide a safe place for people to express their emotions and delve deeper into the truth of their own beings. We looked at this as a gift we had been given to supply a forum for those who had never had such an outlet for expression. The workshops allowed participants to discover the divinity within and help it to surface. We discussed the angelic qualities that we all possess. A large portion of the workshop was devoted to acknowledging intuition, listening to it, following it, and allowing it to assist in guiding people's choices in life.

We also encouraged people to share their angelic experiences or discuss their losses in life or the obstacles they have had to overcome. People were very eager to express their emotions, but so many of them had not felt safe or been encouraged to do so by their cultures. During one workshop, a man from Japan was moved to stand up and share the experience of his mother's passing and how she came to him in a vision. He had been so touched by this experience, but he had never been able to share it before because he did not feel safe. He was brought to tears during his sharing, and he was so grateful that he could now get this episode out in the open.

Something very interesting occurred after one of the workshops we gave. Sandy and I had completed the last segment of the workshop, and we were mingling with some of the guests in the library adjacent to the lecture hall. I was having a conversation with a man when something appeared to be flashing from one of the bookshelves and caught my attention out of the corner of my eye. Still listening to the man speaking, I slightly turned my head to the left to see what this was.

It was a plain white-covered book with an iridescent title on the cover. I realized that this iridescence was reflecting the light directly into my eye. Upon finishing the conversation, I quickly walked over to the bookcase to look at the book. The sole title on the cover was *11:11*. Naturally, I was intrigued, remembering how Deanna had shared with me the special meaning of this number, which she and Tara had so often discussed. I picked up the book and opened it to the title page, which read: *11:11 Inside the Doorway* by Solara. Beneath that title was a pair of angel wings. My curiosity was extremely aroused at this point. As I read the first page, my heart was racing with thoughts of what might have been in Tara's mind on a subconscious level. Some of Solara's key points read: "11:11 is the fulfillment of our Divine Missions upon the earth. It is our bridge to ascension, our doorway Home. 11:11 is about completion, graduation, mastery, empowerment, embodying our Highest Truth, freedom, sacred union, True Love, One Heart, Oneness." As I read this passage, I wondered if this was only a coincidence, or if Tara somehow knew the meaning of this element of time and her destiny.

The fact that I happened to be at this particular workshop, and in this book section, and that this singular book flashed in my eye leads me to believe that there was a message for me that day, or perhaps, a sign from Tara that what we were attempting to do with these work-shops was a continued evolution of her message and our purpose.

We did no advertising for our workshops. Various organizations would call inquiring about our ability to provide a workshop or on the recommendation of others. We found that this was another avenue for getting a message out to many people hungering for it. People would comment to us after each workshop about how much love we emitted when we were conducting these sessions. They were renewed at having the opportunity to be a part of this self-discovery. They wanted more after realizing how special it was to feel and express and learn about themselves. This, too, seemed to be yet another piece of the puzzle that was creating the big picture of the plan in our lives.

During the first few months of 1995, we felt that we had everything under control with the business. Our employees were all in place, and everything appeared to be operating in a comfortable manner. We had always felt very fortunate that we had employees who were so special and important to the success of our venture. Unfortunately, we would be saying good-bye to Tara's friend Jen in the fall, as she was leaving for college. To think of her graduating and moving on was very difficult for both Sandy and me. Tara, of course, would have been graduating with Jen, which stirred up very mixed emotions. Jen had been with us since the inception of the store and was truly irreplaceable.

Thinking about Jen and Tara brought back the memories of Kauai and the wonderful vacation we had spent there, and then the memory of the vacation with Deanna in Kauai. I suddenly had an overwhelming urge to go back to Kauai and really open a store there. I couldn't get this idea out of my mind. If I could have hopped on a plane right then, I would have dropped everything and gone immediately. Sandy and I already had a major trip planned later that year for our twentieth wedding anniversary, so it didn't seem very feasible to plan another excursion to Kauai. But I didn't care. Somehow and some way we were going to Kauai. We had to do it! Interestingly enough, about two weeks later, Deanna went to Sandy and said, "Mom, I really want to go to Kauai. I feel it's some place I need to be. We have to go." Deanna had no knowledge of my feelings or thoughts on this matter. She, too, was having the same feeling of necessity about being back in Kauai. I couldn't get this idea out of my mind. In our kitchen I posted a picture of a private beach we had discovered on our original trip to Kauai, just to act as a constant reminder. I visualized myself being there on the beach. I kept saying to Sandy that we were going to be there sometime that summer.

One week later, when Sandy was working in the store with Jen, Jen approached Sandy and said in an insistent manner, "Sandy, you have got to open a store in Kauai because I have to go there and I can work in the store during the summer. I am very serious. I just have to go back to Kauai " Sandy was astonished at Jen's urgency and determination to go to Kauai after having witnessed my preoccupation with this and Deanna's strong desire. When Sandy shared Jen's conversation with me, I began to wonder what Tara was trying to tell us. It had to be Tara! The fact that this urge had taken over Deanna, Jen, and me was not just a coincidence; there was something else at work here. Sandy and I again began to think very seriously about opening a store in Kauai. We had no doubt it would succeed, and we seemed to have our current stores under control. I believed that my desire for a more peaceful life and being surrounded by nature (which is also a desire that Deanna has voiced many times) was being answered by the universe. We were being given not only a sign but the opportunity to create another existence that would help us find the peace and joy we were seeking in our lives. There would be details to work out logistically, but if this was the right action for us to surrender to, the details would work themselves out. While we still haven't opened our store in Kauai, we know it's only a matter of waiting for the perfect timing.

My mind began to make preparations for our trip to Kauai. I knew deep in my heart that we had to be there sometime around August 18. This would be the third anniversary of Tara's death, and I felt that spending time in the paradise we had shared with Tara would be the perfect way to remember her and reflect on the two life-times we had experienced in those few short years.

Just when things started to calm down, a controversy arose that again put Tara's Angels on the front page of the *Los Angeles Times*. Since we opened the store in 1993, we have carried an angel pin that became the insignia of the store. It's a little gold pin about an inch tall that has become the representation of hope and inspiration for Tara's Angels. After the murder of Nicole Brown Simpson in 1994, her family heard about the loss of our daughter, and they visited the store. Sandy shared the story of Tara with them and gave each of them one of Tara's angel pins. They were so touched that they adopted these pins as a representation of Nicole. They began to purchase the pins in memory of Nicole and give them to people. They had given one of these pins to prosecutor Marcia Clark. When the O.J. Simpson trial began, she started wearing this pin in the courtroom as an expression of support for the family. This sparked a controversy over the appropriateness of such a display. Judge Lance Ito ordered her not to wear the pin in the courtroom, as he felt it was a distraction for the jurors. The next day an article appeared on the front page of the *Los Angeles Times* about the history of the pin as it pertained to Tara's Angels. The phone rang off the hook with orders for the pin. In fact, people began coming in to ask for "the pin" that Marcia Clark was wearing.

This was just another way that Tara had of creating some excitement and getting her name and message out there. I no longer questioned the power of God and the angels and the events that are created in our lives. The experiences of people and their connection with Tara, now that she was part of the consciousness of so many, had become a way of life. I accepted what they had experienced and understood that there was something so magnificent occurring that I did not have the need to validate it as I had in the past. This was a key piece of the puzzle that was now starting to make sense to me.

The lovely family that had purchased the house we were living in at the time of Tara's death approached me one afternoon in the store. They said that they needed to share something very important with me. When they had purchased the house in January 1993, they knew we had lost our daughter. The wife began to share with me how spiritual she had become after moving into the house. I wasn't quite sure what to think of this, but I continued to listen to her experiences. One evening she was awakened by her nine-year-old son, whose bedroom used to be Tara's room. He saw white light flashing throughout the entire room and something that could be equated to a fluttering accompanying this white light. He also heard indescribably beautiful music. He was frightened yet mesmerized by these sights and sounds. When he called for his mother, she came running down the hall, faintly hearing the beautiful music. As she entered the room, she caught a glimpse of the light, which then immediately stopped. They looked out the window, but didn't see or hear anything in the peaceful neighborhood surrounding them. They could not explain this experience, but they knew exactly what had happened. They did not question it, but just accepted it as Tara. They, too, knew the power and presence of angels and had a validation of our experience and the reality of Tara's angels.

I began to wonder if there would ever be an end to the experiences that people were sharing with us about how Tara had influenced their lives. The stories continued to pour in through the mail and in person at the store. I began to feel that I needed to place a protective shell around me so as not to allow myself to be vulnerable to my feelings. I wanted to help others and be there to listen to them in their time of need. I wanted people to feel the hope and inspiration of life here and life after death, knowing that this planet is but a brief stopping place where we can evolve and learn the lessons we need in order to become the purest soul that God intended. God's power is miraculous, and each of us has that power within us to love, create, and make a difference in this world. No matter how large or small the contribution, it can make a difference.

11

My Journey Home

God's love prevails
throughout every moment of our existence.
We learn this as humans
and truly experience it as spiritual beings.

In the spring of 1995, I received a letter from a young woman in Atlanta, Georgia, who was writing on behalf of a male co-worker who had lost his daughter just nine months earlier. She told me how sad and removed he was and asked if I could, perhaps, write to him or call him and shed some hope or peace into his life. She included a poem he had written and a photograph of him opening a gift with a smile. I mention this photograph only to explain what I could see and feel based on my own experience. I could see that his smile was trying to cover up his grief, trying to mask his true devastation. He wanted to go on with his life but didn't know how or even why. Life did not have the same meaning or maybe any meaning. How could it? When what life is all about is suddenly taken from you, what is left—emptiness, a cold, dark place where something once existed but now is void of everything? I read his poem and again looked at the photograph and knew exactly what was going through his mind and his heart. A father's love for his daughter is one of the most precious gifts that life can bestow. When that part of your being is ripped away, it makes you question God, yourself, and all existence. But we all have choices in life. We can't change events, but we can change our perception of these events. This is what makes the difference in how we live our lives—our choice about how we view life. Life is a series of events that lead us from one lesson to the next. Some of us get the lessons, and some of us do not. But that's okay. We can each evolve at our own pace and in our own time. Life can be joyous, or life can be miserable; we make the decision. I believe the Zen Buddhists have the right philosophy: Accept. They believe that we suffer less when we accept experiences without questioning the outcome, knowing that the result is for our highest good. It is what we learn in the process that makes a difference. For if we only anticipate the outcome of a situation and pay no attention to the process, what have we learned? Accept life, move through it, and rejoice in the process. Life is a gift!

A couple of days later, I felt moved to respond to the young woman's request. Unfortunately, I had misplaced the letter. I had so wanted to have contact with this man, knowing the heartbreak that he was feeling, but I couldn't find the letter. I concluded that I was to wait to have contact with him, since the letter was lost or misplaced. When it was right for me to speak to him, the letter would reappear. I was beginning to live my life this way—accepting the natural flow of events. Sometimes I wondered if this was a protective device or if I really believed in this philosophy. I was truly unsure of my feelings. I didn't want any more pain in my life, so I shut down my feelings. I figured that if I didn't "feel," I couldn't be hurt. I started looking at the painful events in my life. They were all centered around loved ones leaving me: my father deserting me at fifteen; my mother dying when I was in my early twenties, and Tara being killed at fifteen. Life can change at any moment, and someone can be taken from you just like that. No wonder I was putting a wall around myself.

What triggered me to evaluate my feelings was a movie Sandy and I saw one evening. We saw *The Bridges of Madison County,* which is a love story about two people who together discover a passion for each other and living life. Seeing their passion and deep-seated lust for life made me realize that I no longer possessed such a passion in my life. Somewhere along the line, my passion for living and loving had ceased to exist. I remembered having those feelings for people and life, but they were now stifled and smothered by the lessons I had experienced. I wanted that passion back.

Tara was so much on my mind at this point that I asked her and the angels for guidance in restoring my feelings and living life in peace. I placed this issue in the hands of the universe, knowing that having acknowledged the absence of my feelings was the beginning of being able to restore them.

As June was approaching, I began thinking of what would have been Tara's eighteenth birthday and her high school graduation. Jen was sharing with us about the Senior Prom and her preparations for graduation and college. When Jen was around, I somehow felt that Tara was present. Sandy and I received an invitation from the high school student counselor, who had known Tara and supported us after Tara's accident, to attend the Senior Awards Night Banquet. She asked if we would make a presentation of a scholarship from the Tara Moore Memorial Scholarship Fund to a designated student. We chose Jen as the recipient. The ironic part was that the awards banquet was on June 7, Tara's eighteenth birthday. I wasn't quite sure how Sandy and I would endure this experience on this particular day, but we knew that it was important that we present the honor to Jen.

Brian, Tara's boyfriend, had arrived in town from Tennessee on June 3. It had been nearly two years since we had seen him. When he came to our door to visit, I noticed how he had matured. He was almost twenty now and looked like a young man. Brian and Tara had been inseparable, and seeing him brought a flood of emotions to my heart. It felt comfortable having him around the way he used to be. I began to wonder what Tara would have looked like at eighteen—how she would have matured and how she might have changed. Brian was a welcome sight that encouraged beautiful memories of the past. How might things have turned out if events had been different? As Sandy, Deanna, Brian, and I all chatted, my mind played games by constantly asking "what if" questions. Once again, I felt the loss and the loneliness, but I made sure that I didn't show it. I had gotten good at masking my inner turmoil.

Having these emotions stirred up, I gave some thought to seeing Dr. Marillyn Brame for another session of hypnotherapy. Ever since the discovery of my near-death experience, I had a knowing that there was still a piece of the puzzle that I hadn't located. There was still something to be found out while I was unconscious during the ambulance ride to the hospital when I was nine years old. I felt that now was the time that I needed to research this episode in my life. Dr. Brame had moved, although I was hopeful that I could locate her.

Once I located Dr. Brame, I called her and said that I was interested in seeing her again, but I didn't explain why. We set the appointment for the next week, and I could hardly wait. When I arrived, Marillyn motioned for me to sit in her recliner. We carried on some small talk for a few minutes, and then I began explaining to her why I had returned. I told her that the last session we had, which was over a year ago, did not disclose all the information that I felt had taken place. I told her that I wanted her to take me deeper if necessary so that I could find out what had occurred between the time I was placed in the ambulance and the time I was revived at the hospital. Everything else was so clear to me, but I knew that there was something else in this experience that I had not yet recalled. I wanted to be taken back to the moment when I was viewing my body from high above—that moment when I was dead.

Marillyn told me to get comfortable as she began playing some soft, relaxing music. She told me to close my eyes and take some deep breaths. Inhale. Exhale. Inhale. Exhale. Then she told me in my mind's eye to go to that very tranquil tropical beach that I loved so much and feel the breeze and hear the waves pounding on the shore. I felt comfortable with Marillyn leading me to this deep, relaxed state. She was very cautious and safe in her procedure. I was very relaxed and ready to begin this journey, even if the destination was unknown.

Marillyn continued to take me deeper until she could see that I was totally relaxed and content in my surroundings. She had me visualize my time line and then suggested that I return to the incident that had occurred when I was nine years old. I quickly responded to her request, and the scene that had played over and over in my mind for most of my life was again so vivid. There I was, observing my mother in her pink dress with the tiny gray stripes talking to the policeman with tears streaming down her face. I saw the ambulance pull into the driveway. As my body was being placed on a stretcher, the back doors of the ambulance were being opened in preparation for this motionless boy to be placed inside. Once I was inside, I experienced what appeared to be a fade-out, like in the movies, and then total darkness.

But wait a minute, there was something else going on here. This wasn't darkness, just the absence of light. I was feeling different. I had an overwhelming feeling I could hardly find words to describe. I was speechless. I was in awe. I loved what I felt and where I was. There was no weight to my body or my soul, just an eerie lightness to my being. Although I was surrounded by what appeared to be darkness, I felt a total feeling of unconditional love. I could not hold back the tears. This feeling was so incredible and the peace and acceptance I felt were so strong that my tears were tears of complete joy and happiness. I was in a place that I did not want to leave, a place where glorious feelings permeated my entire being. I was crying so hard by this time that I could hardly speak.

Suddenly, my head was thrust back as I felt my body or my soul being pushed through the universe at what appeared to be an uncanny speed. I felt as if I were in a vacuum being sucked away into the vastness of the never-ending universe. I wasn't alone. There were other forces around me. They were angels. They did not possess distinct form, but my soul recognized their energy. I was in the company of loving, accepting beings who were supporting me and escorting me on my miraculous journey. There was communication, but not as we know it. There was simply a knowingness of everything without the thought process that we go through. There was only good and love and every positive feeling. My head continued to remain as if it were being pushed back from the intense force of propelling upward, but it was a comforting feeling. I marveled at how the universe was so infinite, with no beginning and no end. This feeling of intense love remained with me as I continued to be bathed in my own tears. I had never felt anything like this in my life. I wanted to remain in this euphoric state forever. I had no concern about where I was going or where I had been. Nothing mattered except how I was feeling that moment. I could see in the far distance a crest of light that I seemed to be heading toward, although it never appeared that I was getting any closer. I was simply basking in this perfect moment with no thought of anything else. I felt that I was home, in a place I belonged and had missed deeply for a long time. There was no fear, no concern, no confusion. I was where I was supposed to be.

Then, I began to feel the pressure on my head gently lessen as the intensity of my journey came to an end. I received a thought coming from some energy force, my angels. I had to go back. I couldn't stay. There was work for me to do, and I had to return. This was the first time on this journey that I felt something other than complete joy and peace. I was disappointed at the statement. I wanted to stay. But a knowledge filled my soul, causing me to realize that there was a reason I had to return to my life on Earth. It was unfortunate that this knowledge would lie buried within me for so many years. Or, perhaps, it was better this way. If I had retained the wisdom of this journey and carried it with me throughout my years, it might have been more painful to live with the sorrows and lessons that accompany life. With the thought of ending my miraculous journey through the universe, my euphoria came to a halt and I surrendered to my destiny—to remain in this plane of existence to carry out some mission. There really wasn't a decision to be made. I acknowledged the request and did what I had to do without questioning. It was part of the plan, another piece of the puzzle.

Marillyn sensed my disappointment at having to return, but she knew that my journey was complete. She gradually brought me back to my normal state of mind. As she studied my reaction to this experience, she looked at me with a proud smile and a glow of success. I sat there processing what had just occurred; what I had actually experienced thirty-four years before had been lying dormant in me all this time. We hugged and said our good-byes, knowing we would be in contact again soon.

As I drove away and reflected on what had happened, I began feeling depressed about having had to leave my spiritual home, a place where there was no judgment, no fear, and only love, peace, and a feeling of joy. It was such a safe place to be—sheltered from life as we experience it here on Earth in human form. I think we forget when we come into this existence that we are all spiritual beings and pure, divine expressions of God. We come here to learn the lessons we need most, and our time is brief. Then, when we return to our spiritual home, we experience the freedom we have searched a lifetime for. If we can learn to live on Earth as the true spiritual beings we really are, enjoying our human qualities, the lessons are fewer and the experience is more rewarding.

The truth of this realization was crucial to my ability to accept my humanness and life as it was at that time. Understanding my true spiritual nature and how the soul interacts on both levels of the universe has enabled me to deal with life and death with a new awareness. I have learned that love never dies. Love, like our souls, is energy, and energy is ongoing and infinite, like the universe. Love transcends all time and space. It is the purest quality that we each possess. This eternal love is, perhaps, the piece of the puzzle that has completed the picture of life the most for me. I have discovered that there are still some pieces missing, because the picture gets bigger the more I discover about myself, but I can now find the pieces more easily. I have come to understand that there is no life or death, just a continuation of our soul's journey.

12

Graduation Day

God creates miracles,
angels make them happen,
and we experience them
so we can believe.

The weather was gorgeous on Tara's eighteenth birthday,
June 7, 1995. We anticipated the Senior Awards Banquet
that evening, almost as if Tara herself were graduating.
We decided to skip work that day and arrange for Deanna
to miss school, and we all went to Disneyland to celebrate. It was a perfect day. The three of us were bonded
together as we laughed our way through the Magic King-
dom. We thought of Tara often, although we did not
speak of her. I could see it in Sandy and Deanna's face,
and feel it in my heart. There is no doubt that she was
there with us in our minds. It was her day and our family outing, just like the ones we used to have.

Tara's Angels

That evening at the awards banquet as we were waiting backstage to present Jen with the scholarship, one of
Deanna's teachers walked over to us to say how much
she appreciated and loved the glass angel that Deanna
had given her as a gift some months ago. She told us
how touched she was by this gesture. Then she asked if
we were holding up okay under the circumstances. We
said yes, and she went on to say how brave Sandy and I
were to be doing this tonight. She started to cry and
had to leave. Suddenly, our names were called, and we
walked onstage. Sandy started her introduction by saying, "It's an honor to be here this evening presenting this
scholarship. As you know, this would have been Tara's
senior year, but she had to graduate a little early because
she had some very important work to do elsewhere. It
also happens to be her eighteenth birthday today." A sub-
tle gasp sounded from the audience, followed by the
falling of tears. Sandy continued. "Tara would be very
proud of the recipient of this scholarship." I then began
my portion of the introduction: "This girl, whom we
have watched blossom into a remarkable young lady, has
been with our store since its inception nearly two years
ago. She was our first and our best employee and will be
greatly missed when she goes off to college. Whenever
she is around, I feel the presence of Tara. It is my privi-
lege to present this scholarship to Jen Farris."

Jen came running up on stage and gave Sandy and me
a hug, and we all cried. As we started to leave the stage,
Francis Griffith, the high school student counselor who
had been presiding, told us to remain onstage as she
wanted to say a few words. She looked at us and then
turned to the audience and began. "When I attended
Tara's memorial service, I remember Sandy saying how
she wanted that day to be Tara's eighteenth birthday, her
high school graduation, and all those special occasions.
Well, today is Tara's eighteenth birthday and her graduation." Francis then asked the audience to stand. As a
birthday cake with eighteen candles was ushered onstage, she requested that everyone sing "Happy Birthday"
to Tara. Sandy and I were deeply touched by this moment
and could not hold back our tears. Then we were presented with a scrapbook that Francis and some of the
senior class had put together. Francis spoke. "Sandy and
Kirk, this book contains some letters written by her
classmates about Tara and a graduation program, a Class
of 95 tassle from the graduation cap and gown, and an
award certificate presented to Tara Moore, the winner of
the Most Beautiful and Spiritual Angel Award." We could
hardly contain ourselves. Tara was there that night and
had graduated with her class and was able to celebrate
her eighteenth birthday with her friends. The room was
filled with pure love. This was a miraculous moment—

a moment we will never forget. This day and this night were a gift to Tara and a gift to us. Love never dies. Tara, we love you!

Epilogue:
There Are Real Angels

We received a very special gift in June 1994 that touched us deeply. It was a poem in a beautiful frame that was sent to us anonymously by an individual who was moved to write it after seeing our story on television.

Touch of an Angel

Your life here on Earth
Was painfully brief.
An untimely passing
Leaves an aura of grief.

But love has remained
That transcends any dream.
'Tis the beauty of light
From an angelic beam.

We're bathed in affection
From a warmth in its glow.
It walks us through trials
And bids us to know.

That though you've departed,
You'll always be near.
The feeling surrounds us
With your message so clear:

There Are Real Angels

157

If you are interested in receiving information about lectures and workshops offered by Kirk Moore and his family, please contact him at the store address below. Catalogs are also available upon request.

Kirk Moore is interested in hearing from you as he works on his second book. And, of course, feel free to stop by and experience the magic of Tara's Angels:

Tara's Angels
31770 Camino Capistrano
San Juan Capistrano, CA 92675
(714) 248-7277

ALSO FROM H J KRAMER

MESSENGERS OF LIGHT:
The Angels' Guide to Spiritual Growth
by Terry Lynn Taylor
Learn how to spot angels, communicate with them,
utilize their help, and love life the way they do.

CREATING MIRACLES:
Understanding the Experience of Divine Intervention
by Carolyn Miller, Ph.D.
Discover the book where science and miracles meet!
The first scientific look at creating miracles in your life.
These simple practices and true stories offer new wisdom
for accessing the miraculous in daily life.

THE LAWS OF SPIRIT:
Simple, Powerful Truths for Making Life Work
by Dan Millman
A book of timeless values, containing twelve
universal principles for living and loving well.
From the author of *Way of the Peaceful Warrior.*

UNDERSTAND YOUR DREAMS:
1500 Dream Images and How to Interpret Them
by Alice Anne Parker
The essential guide to becoming your own dream expert—
makes dreaming a pleasure and waking an adventure.

INTO A TIMELESS REALM:
A Metaphysical Adventure
by Michael J. Roads
Australian author Michael Roads explores the links
between nature, evolution, consciousness, and time.

TO ORDER BOOKS, PLEASE CALL (800) 833-9327